Swear Words COLORING BOOK

BELONGS TO:

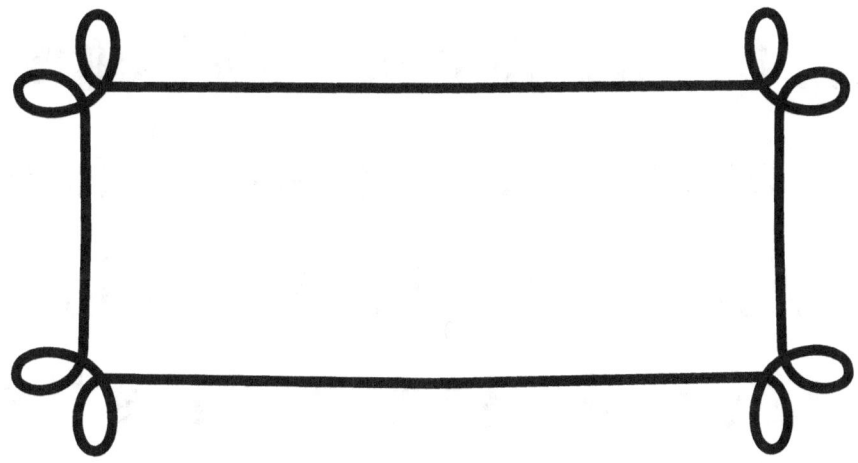

COPYRIGHT© 2024 HAPPY FIELD
ALL RIGHTS RESERVED

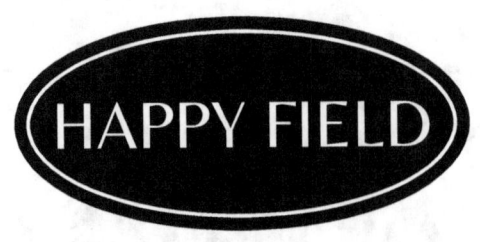

We hope you're enjoying your purchase! If you have a moment, please leave us a review on Amazon.

Your feedback not only helps us improve but also assists other customers in making informed decisions.

It's quick, simple, and means a lot to us.

Thank you for choosing our Swear Words Coloring Book!

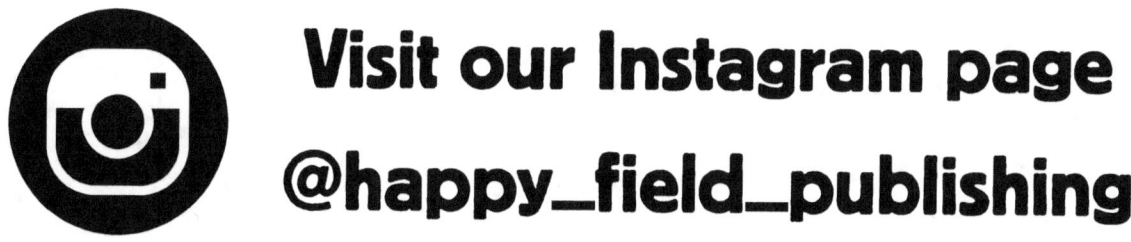

Visit our Instagram page
@happy_field_publishing

just scan the QR code:

Share your finished artworks with us!

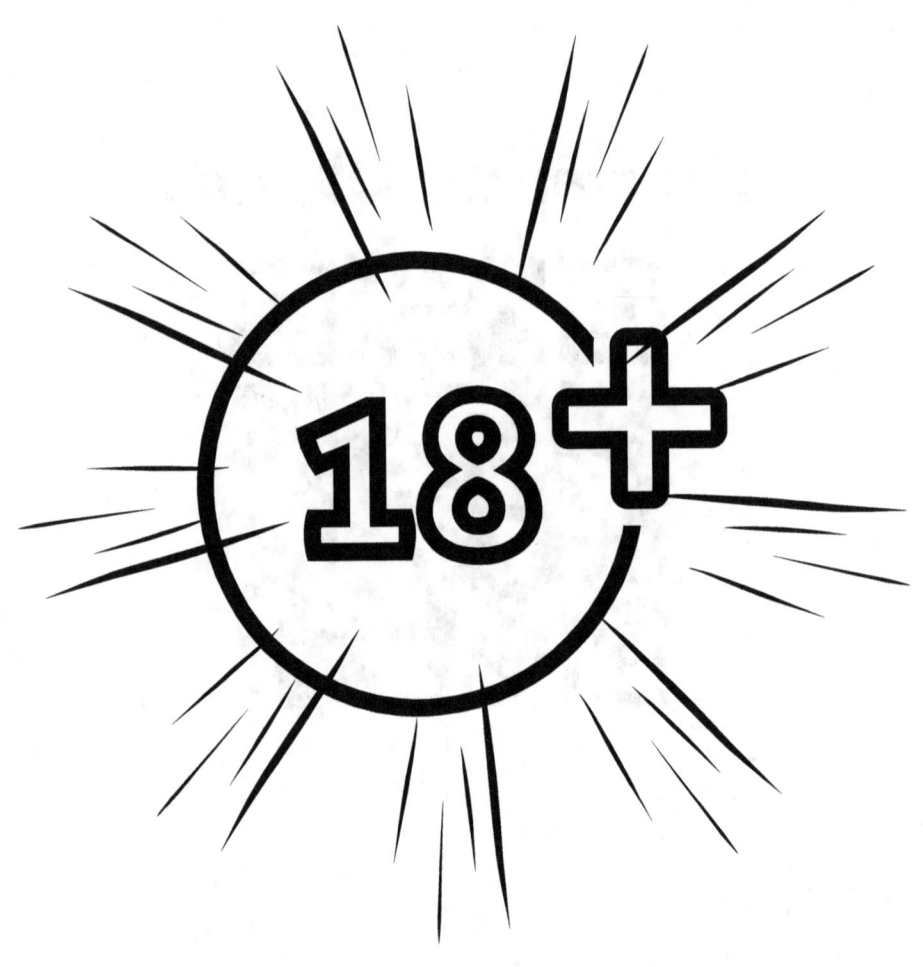

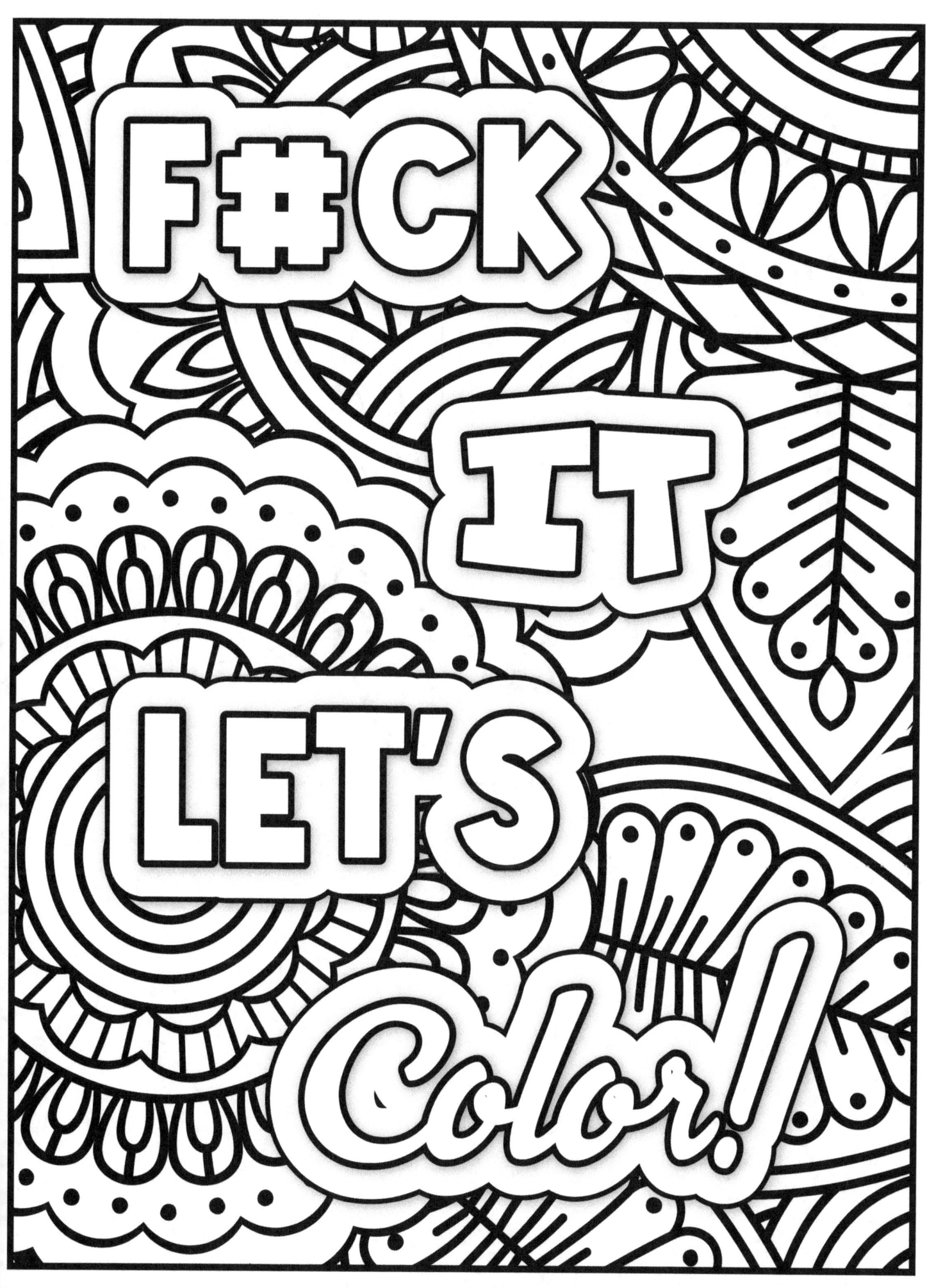

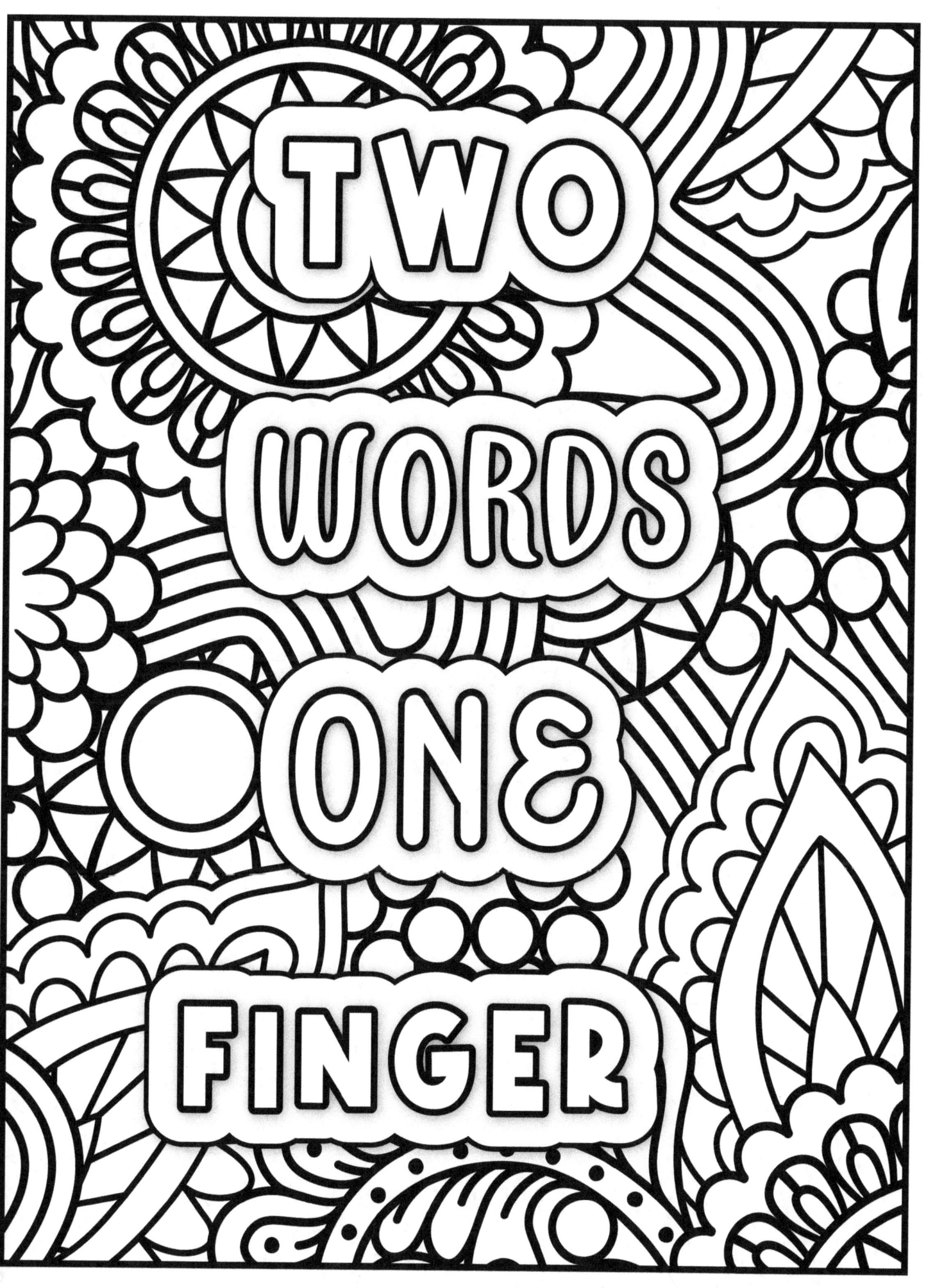

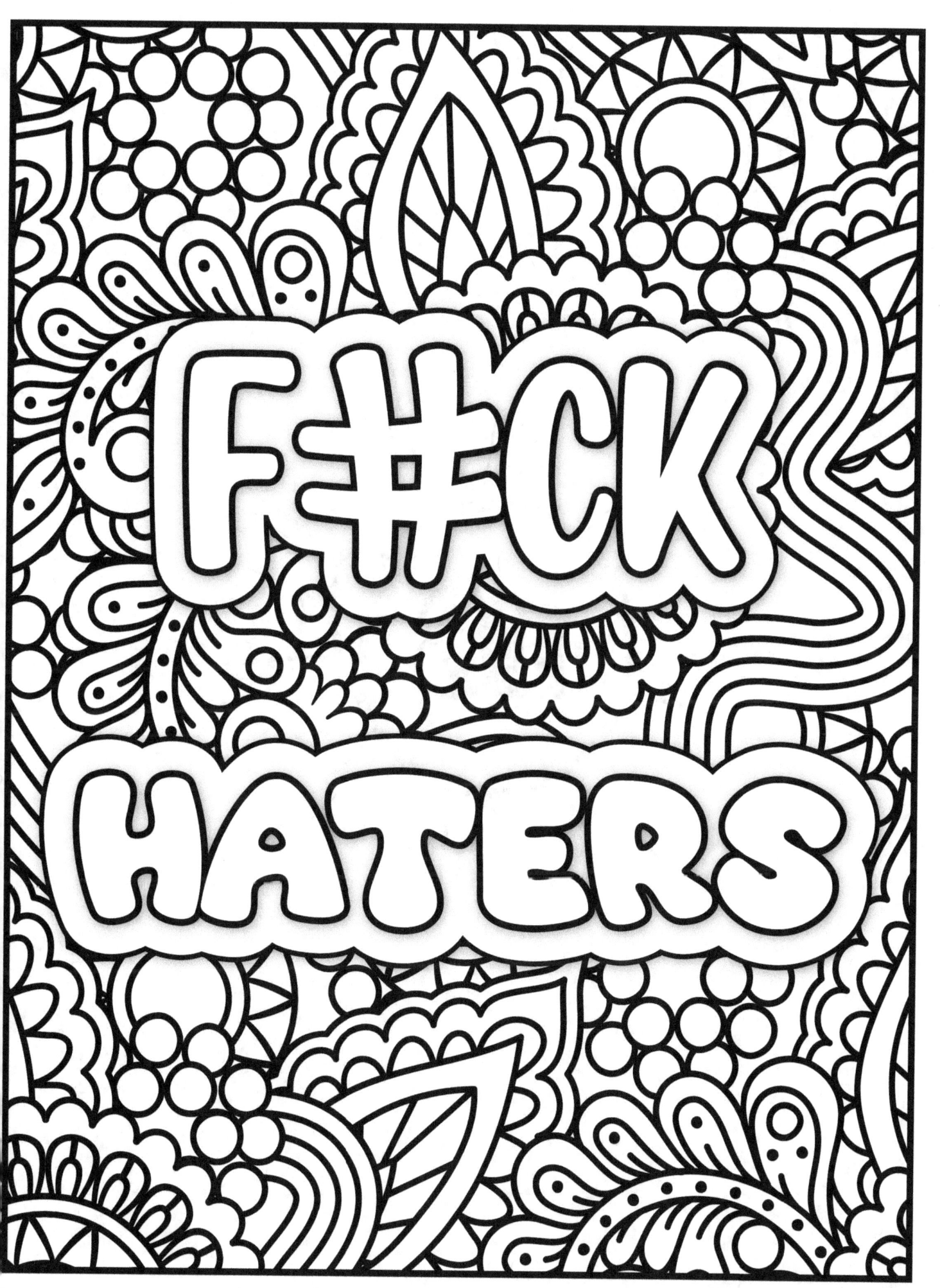

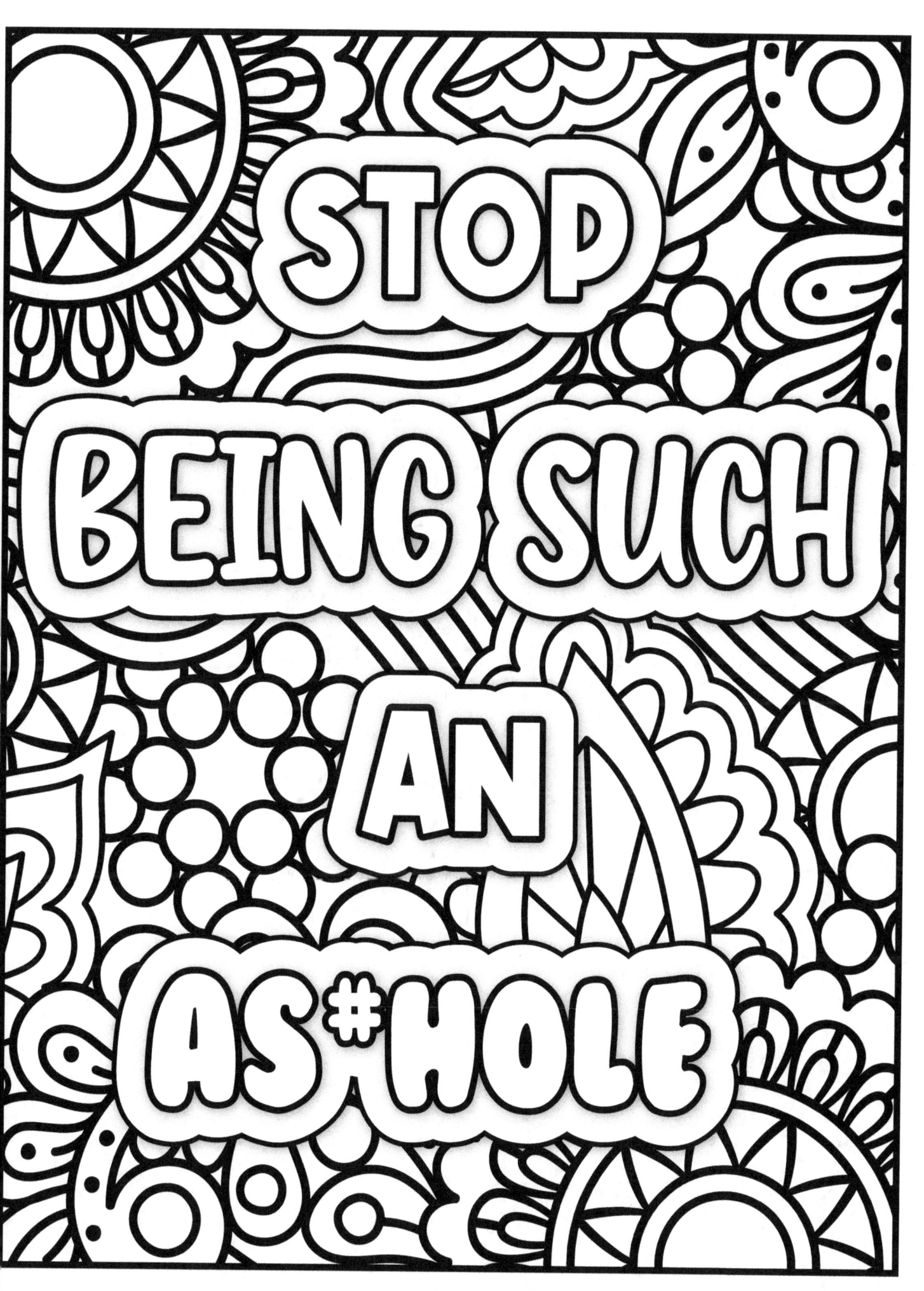

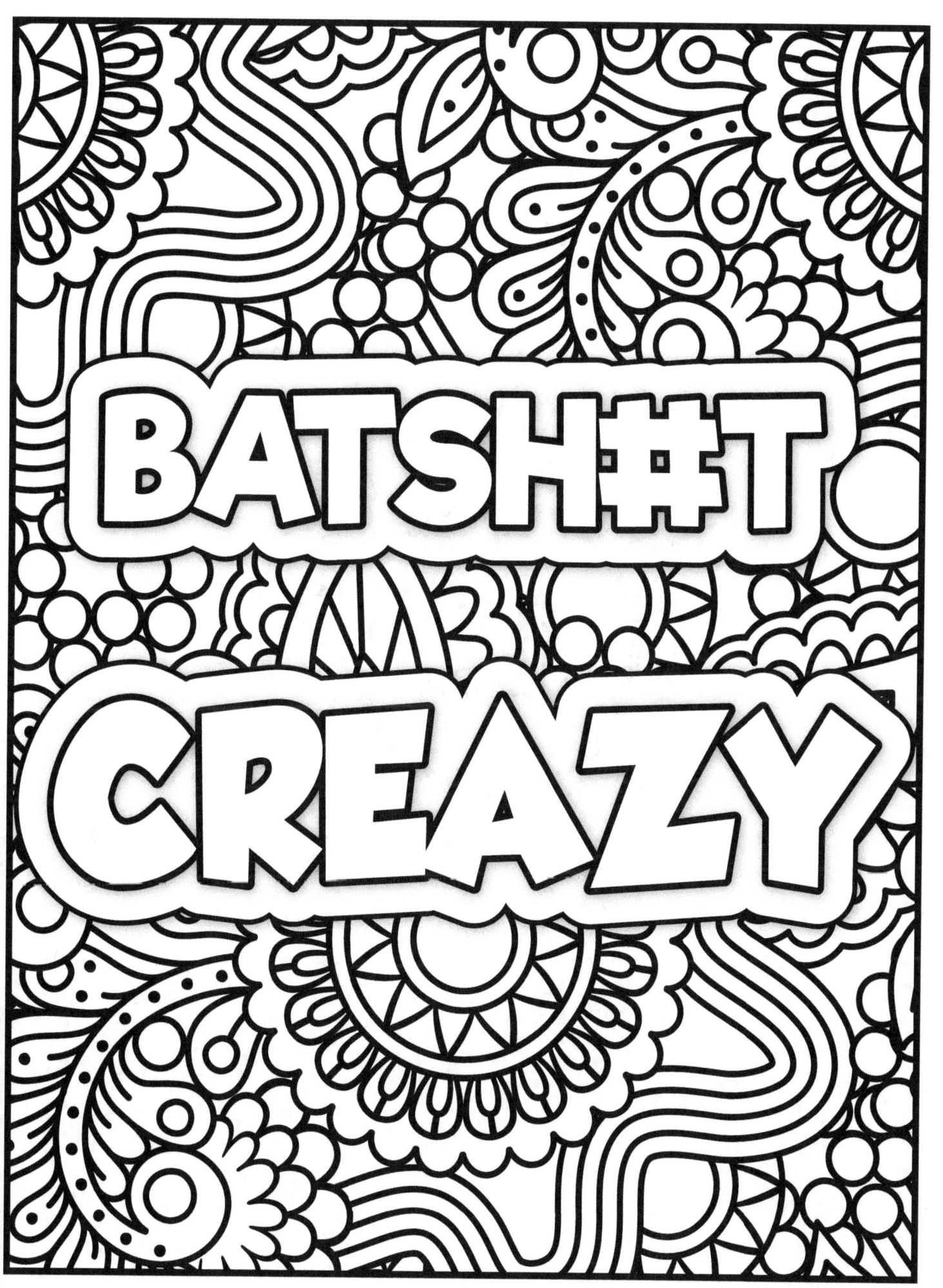

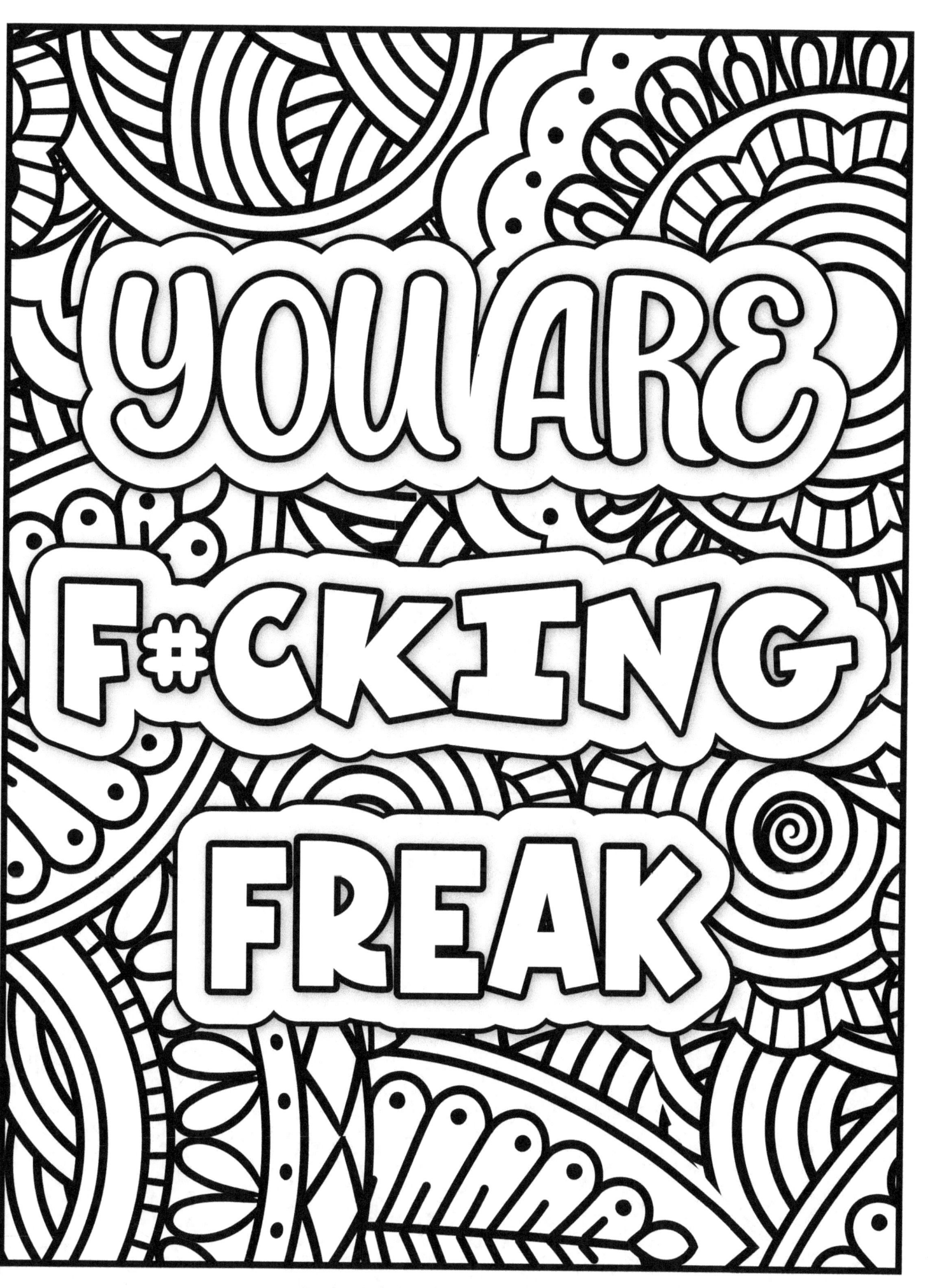

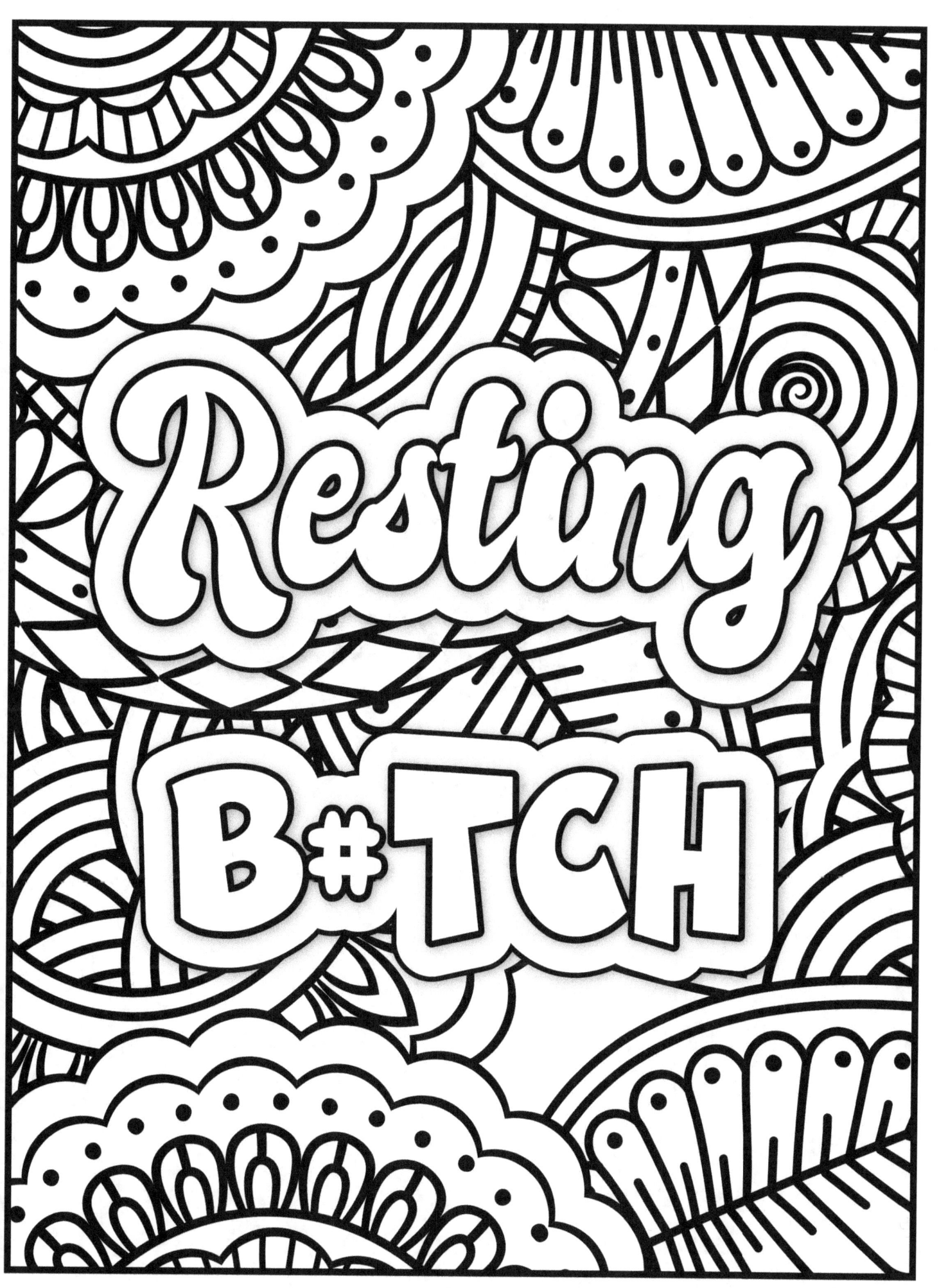

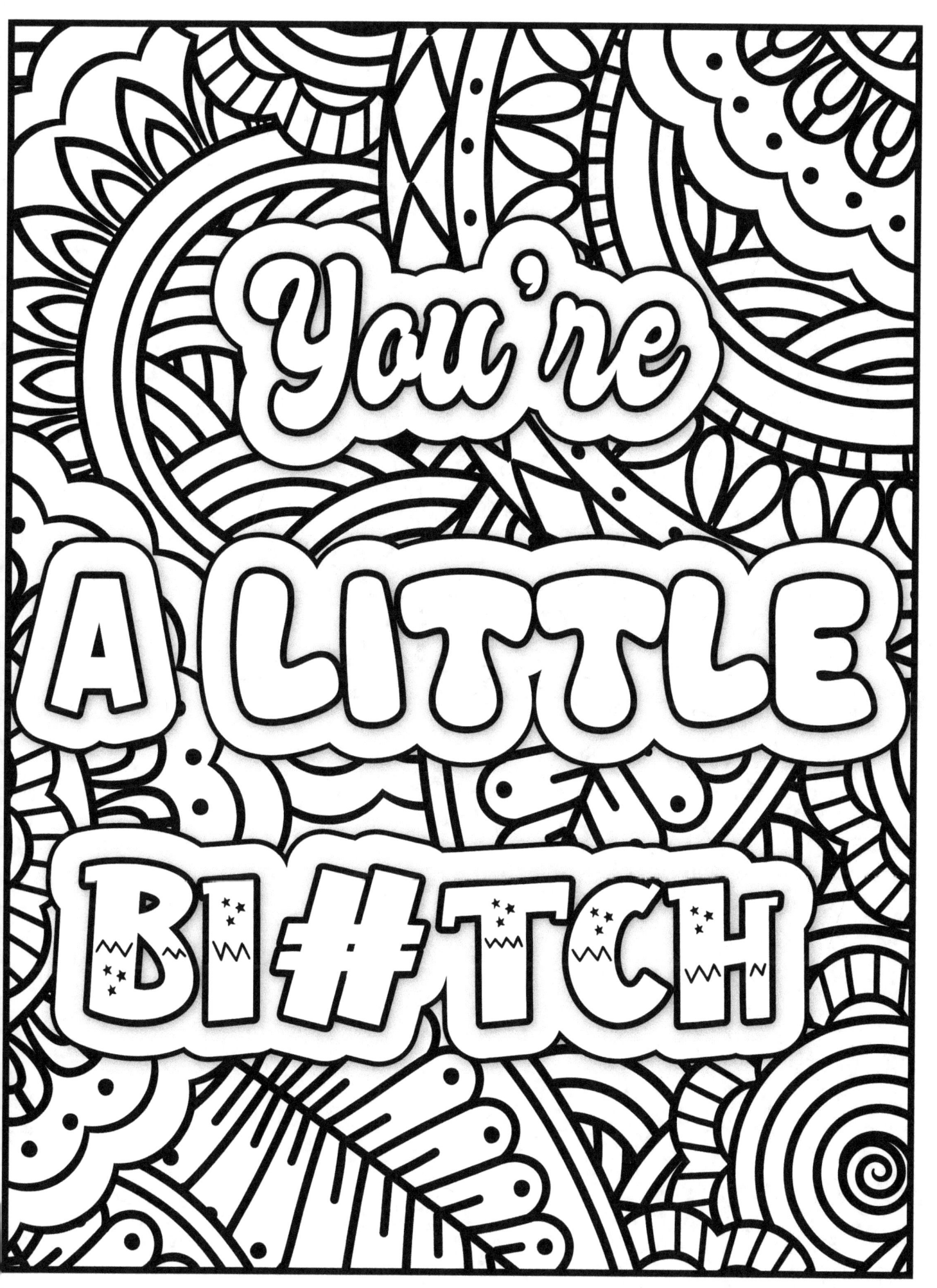

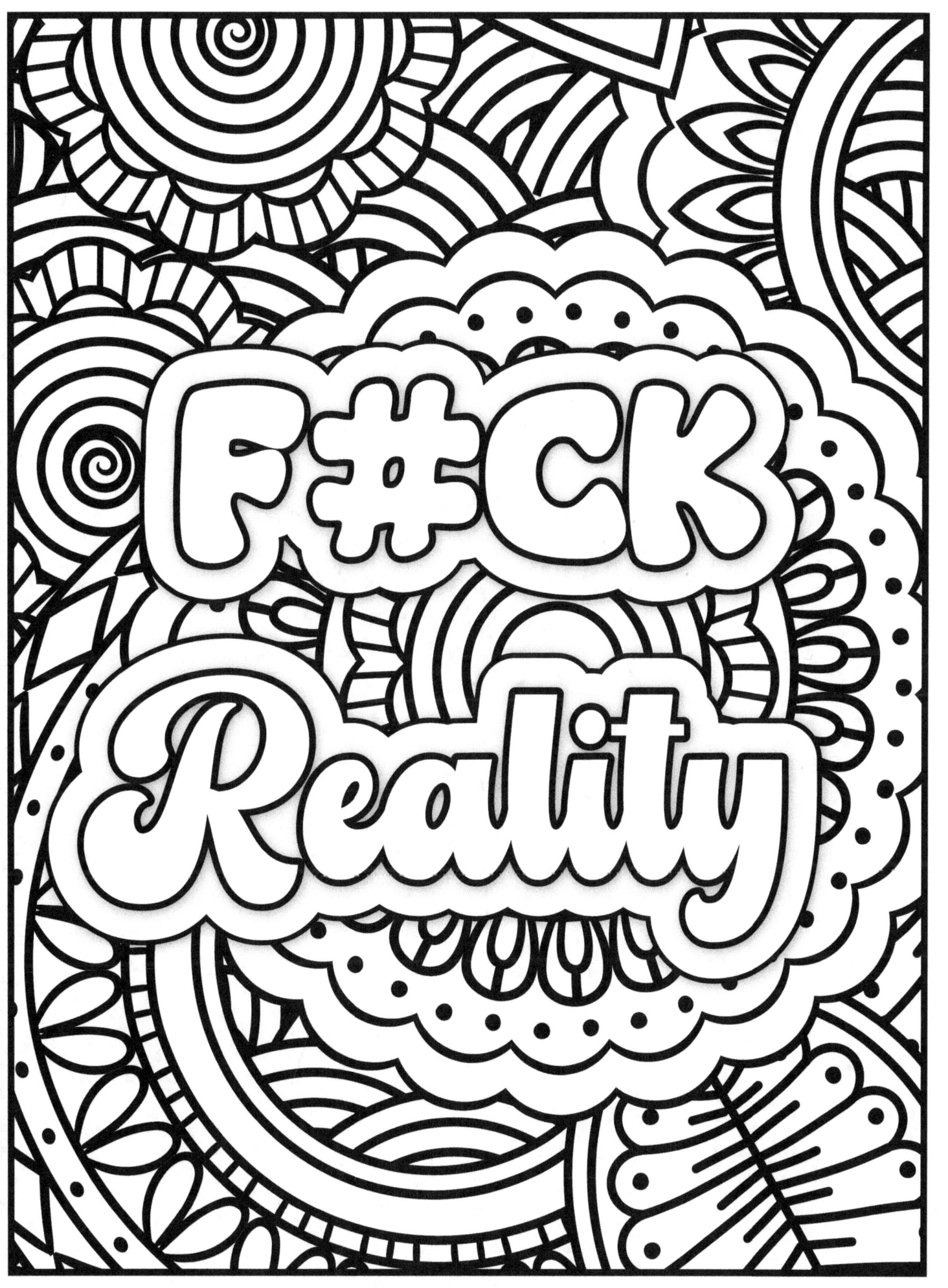

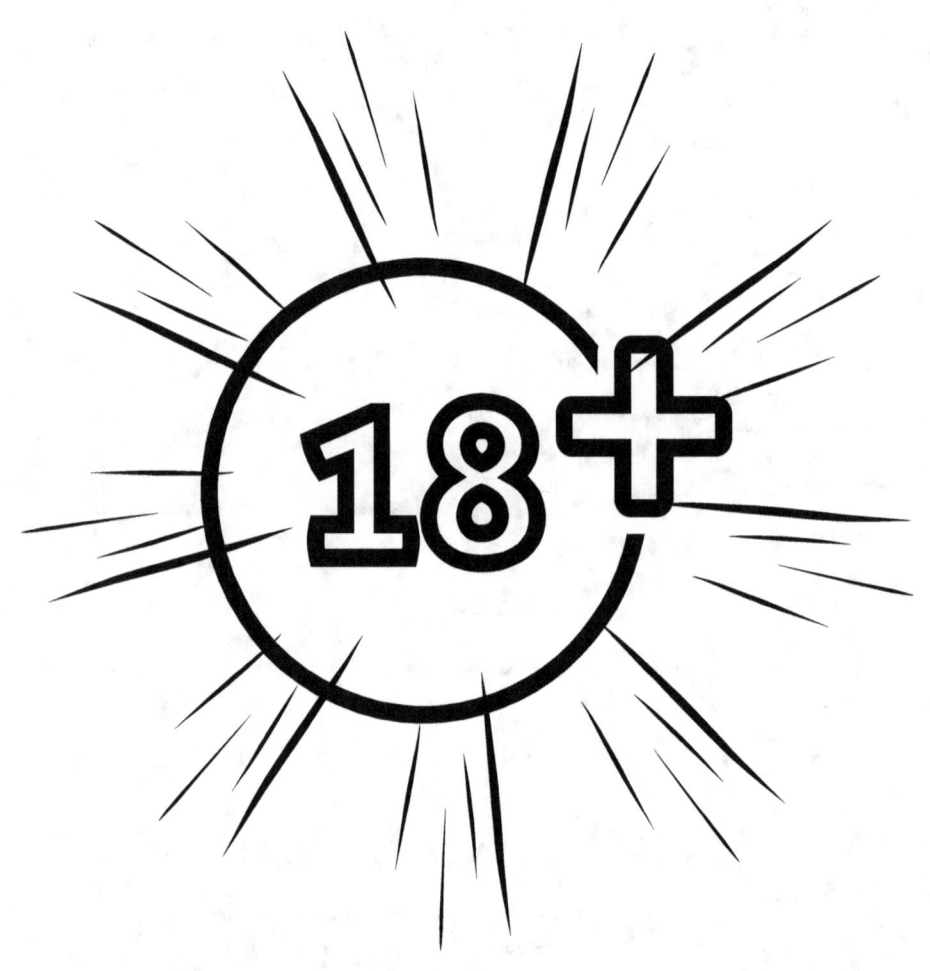

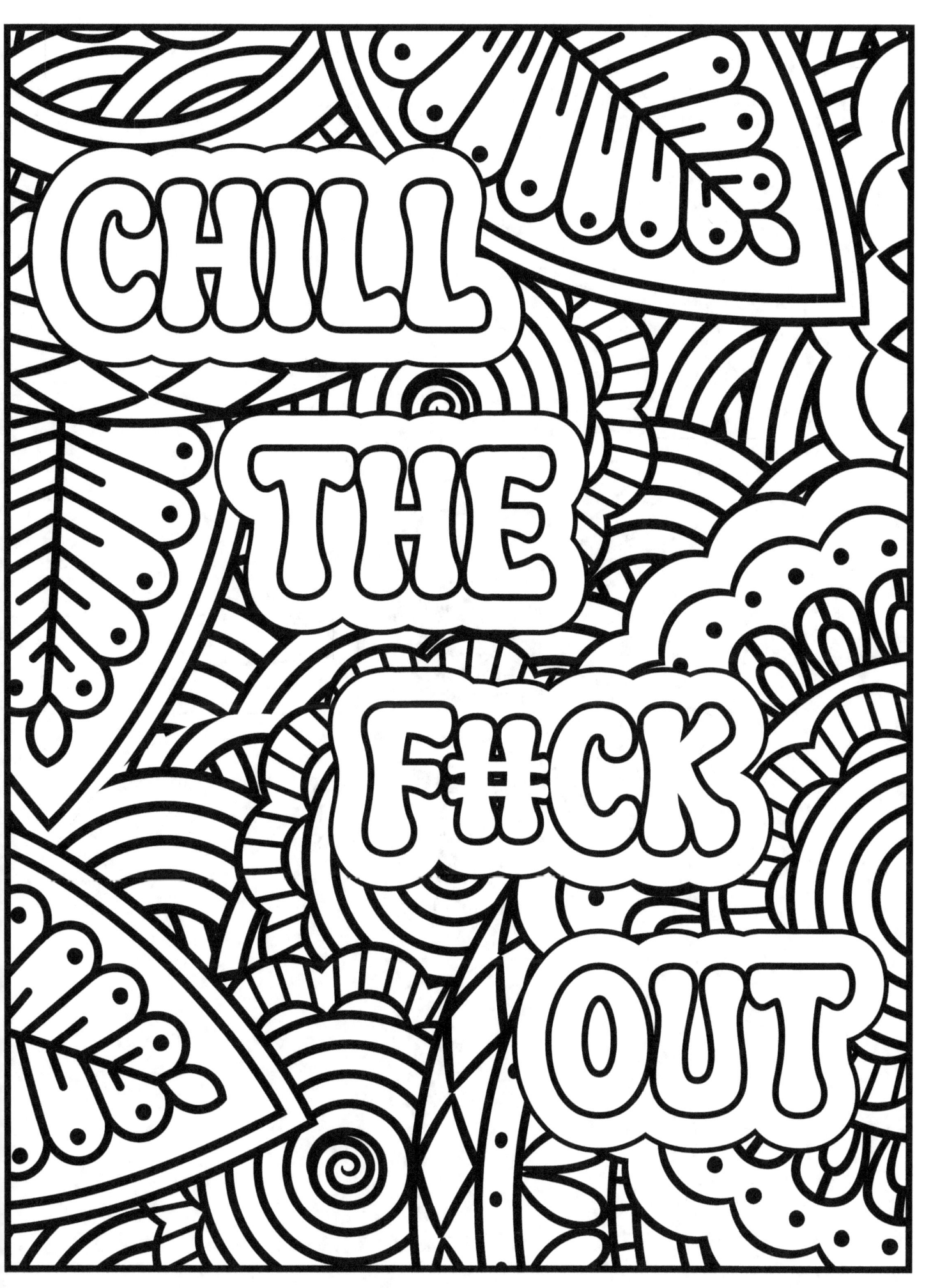

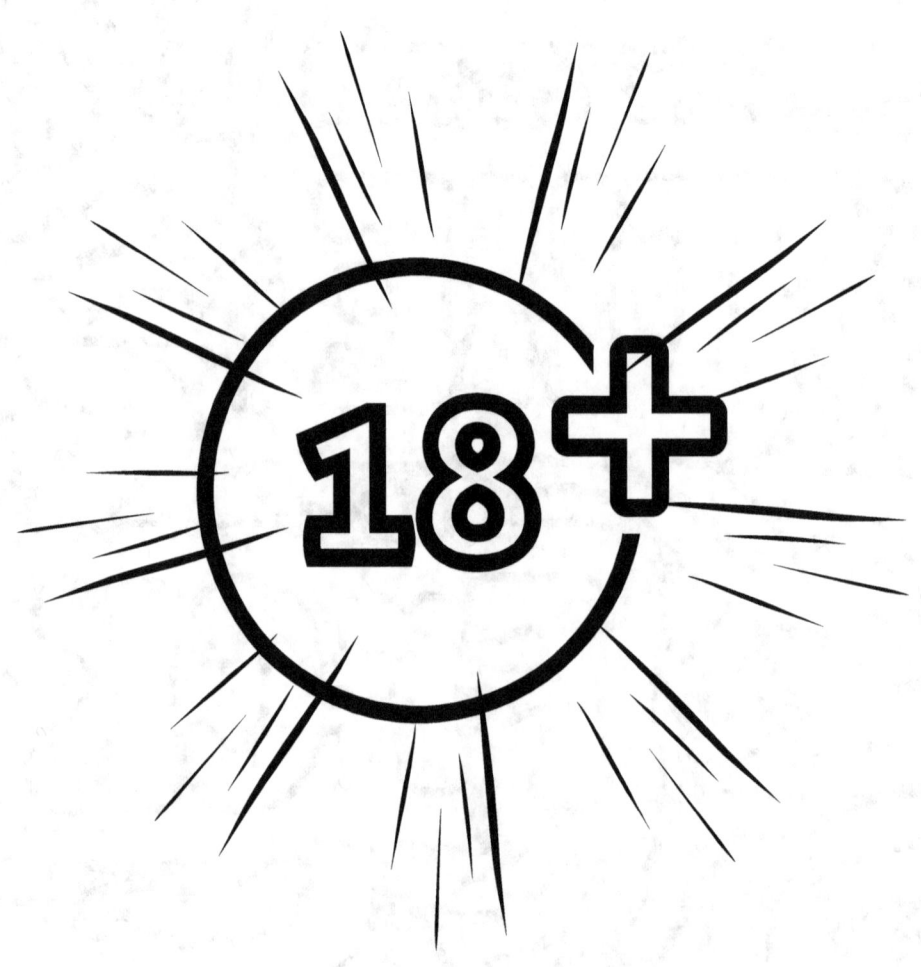

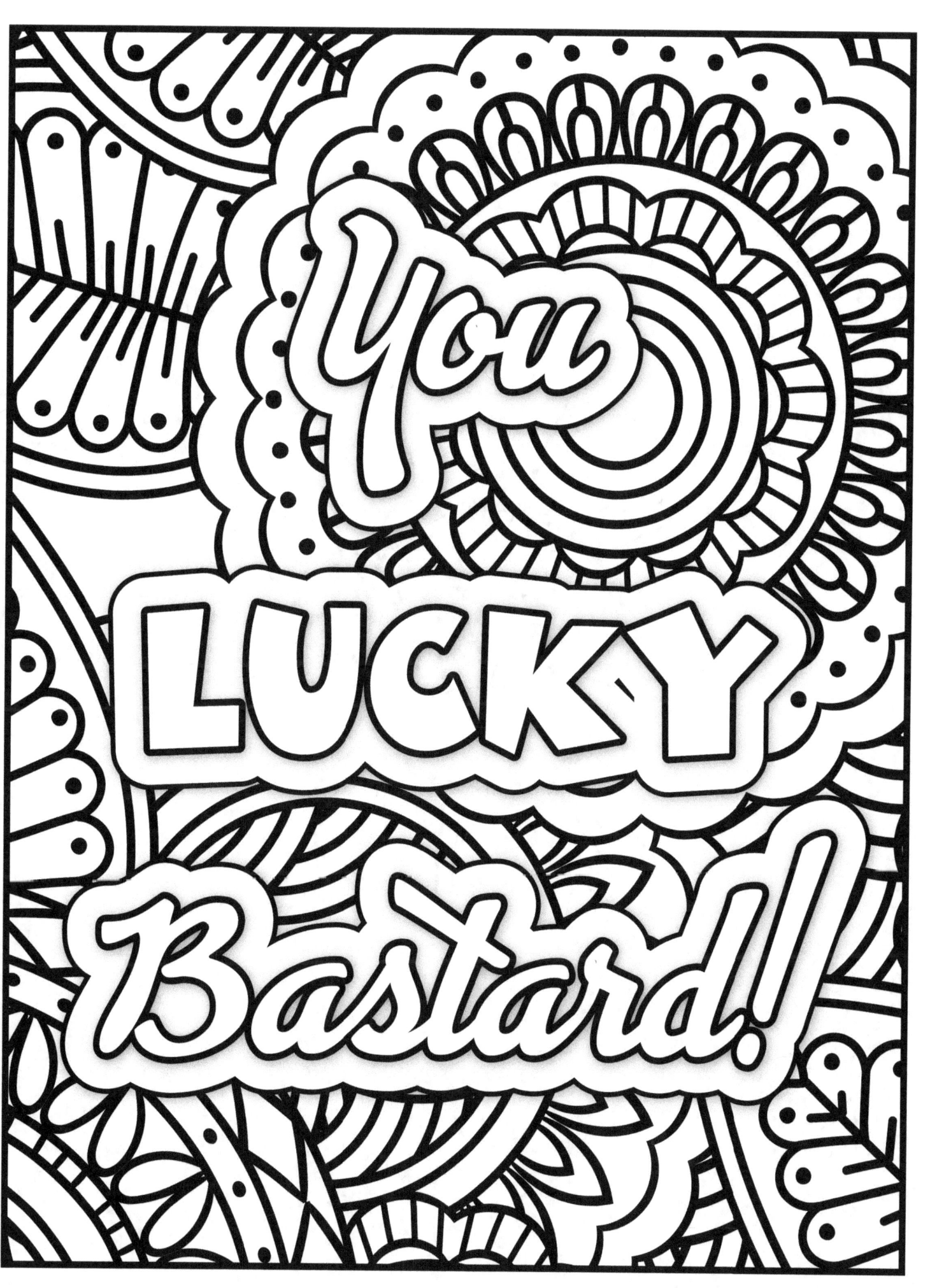

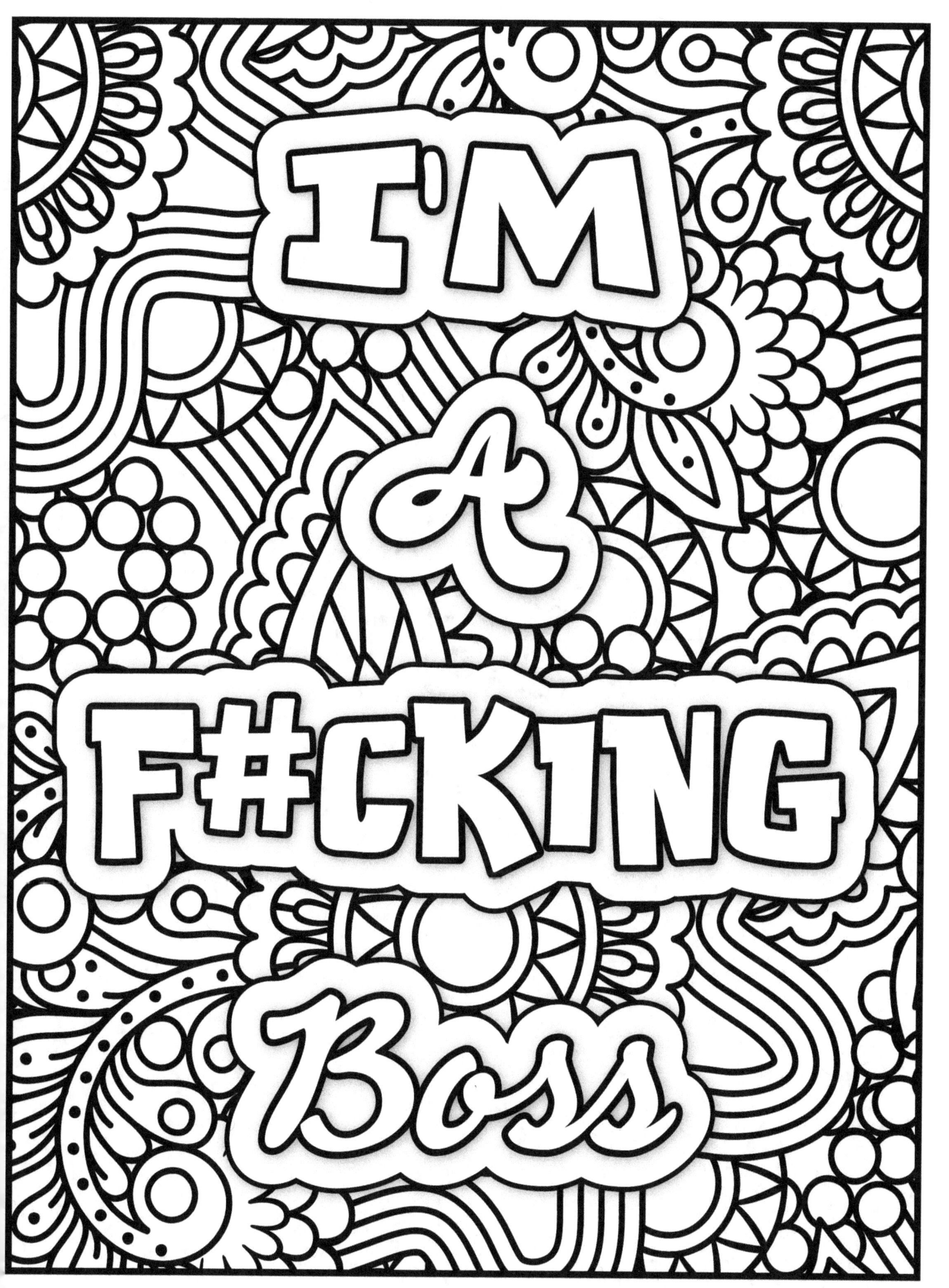

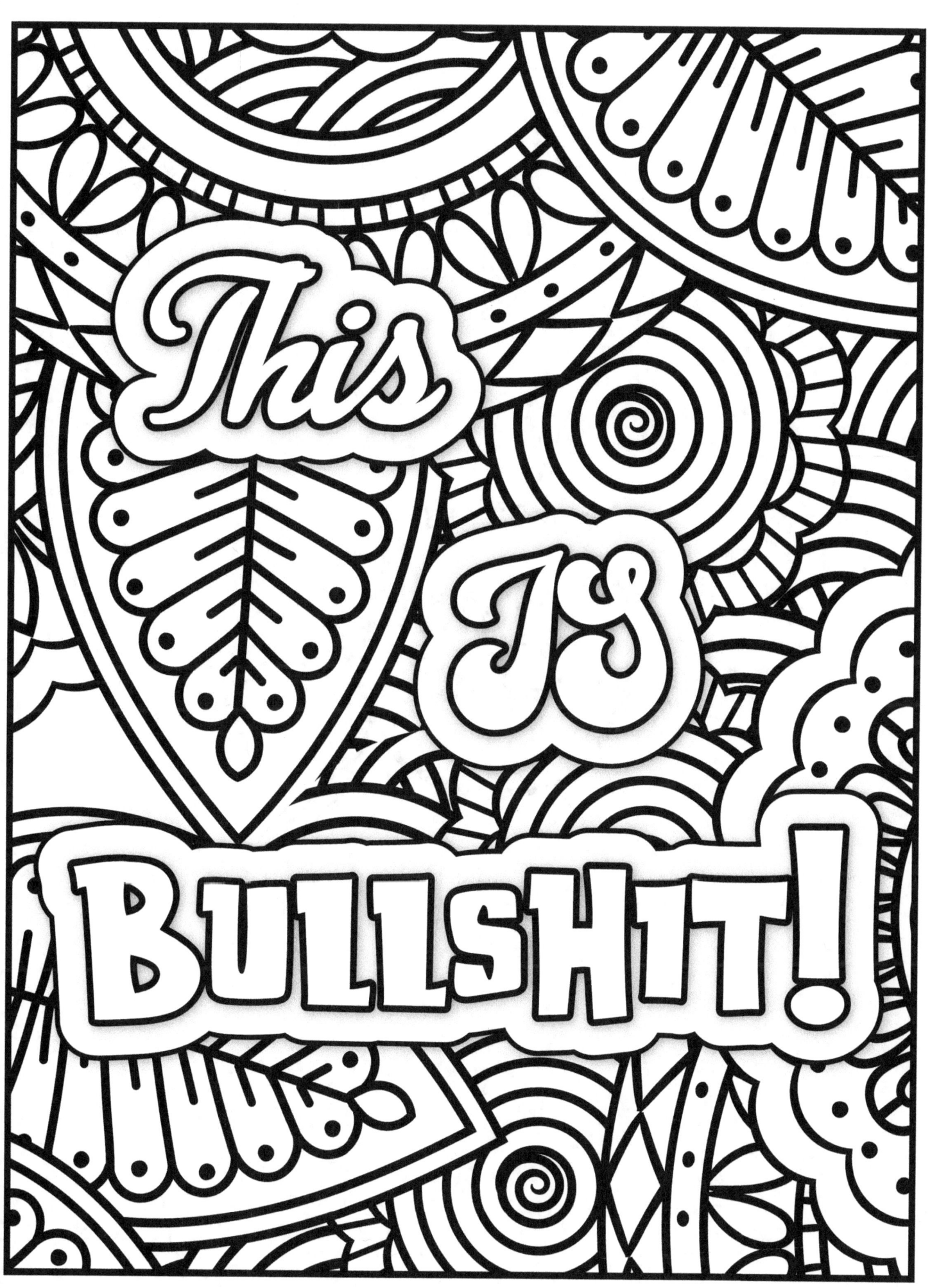

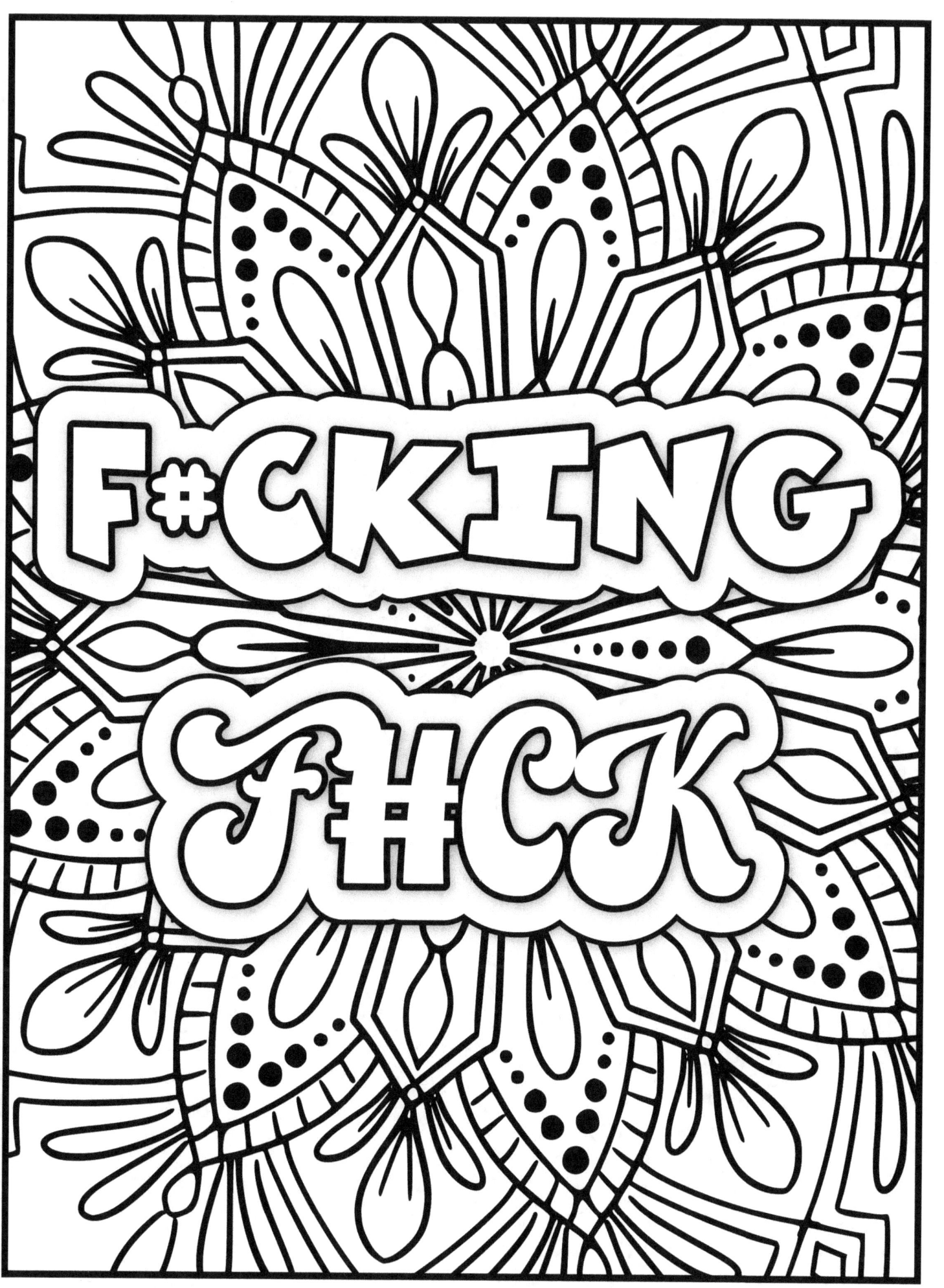

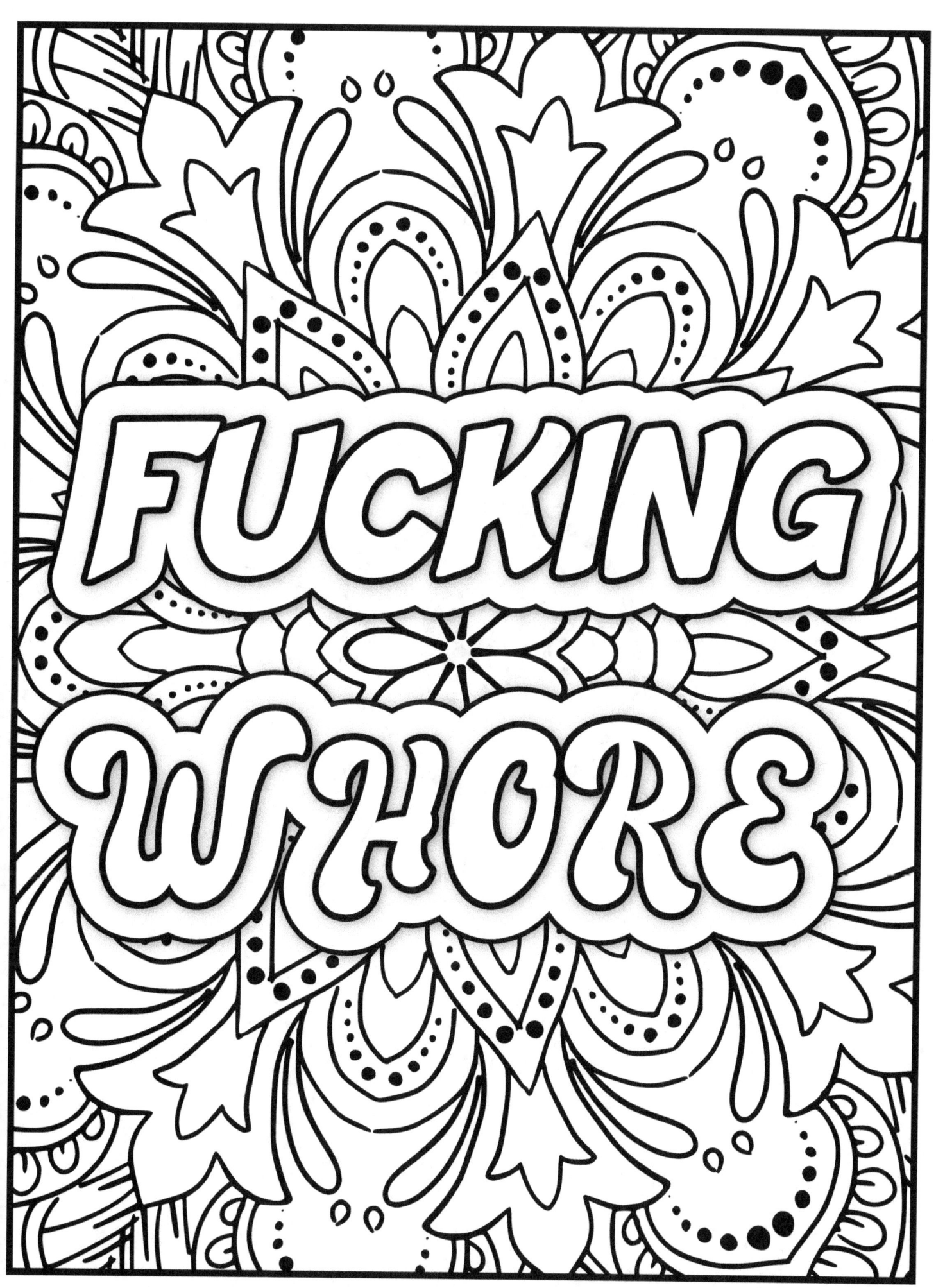

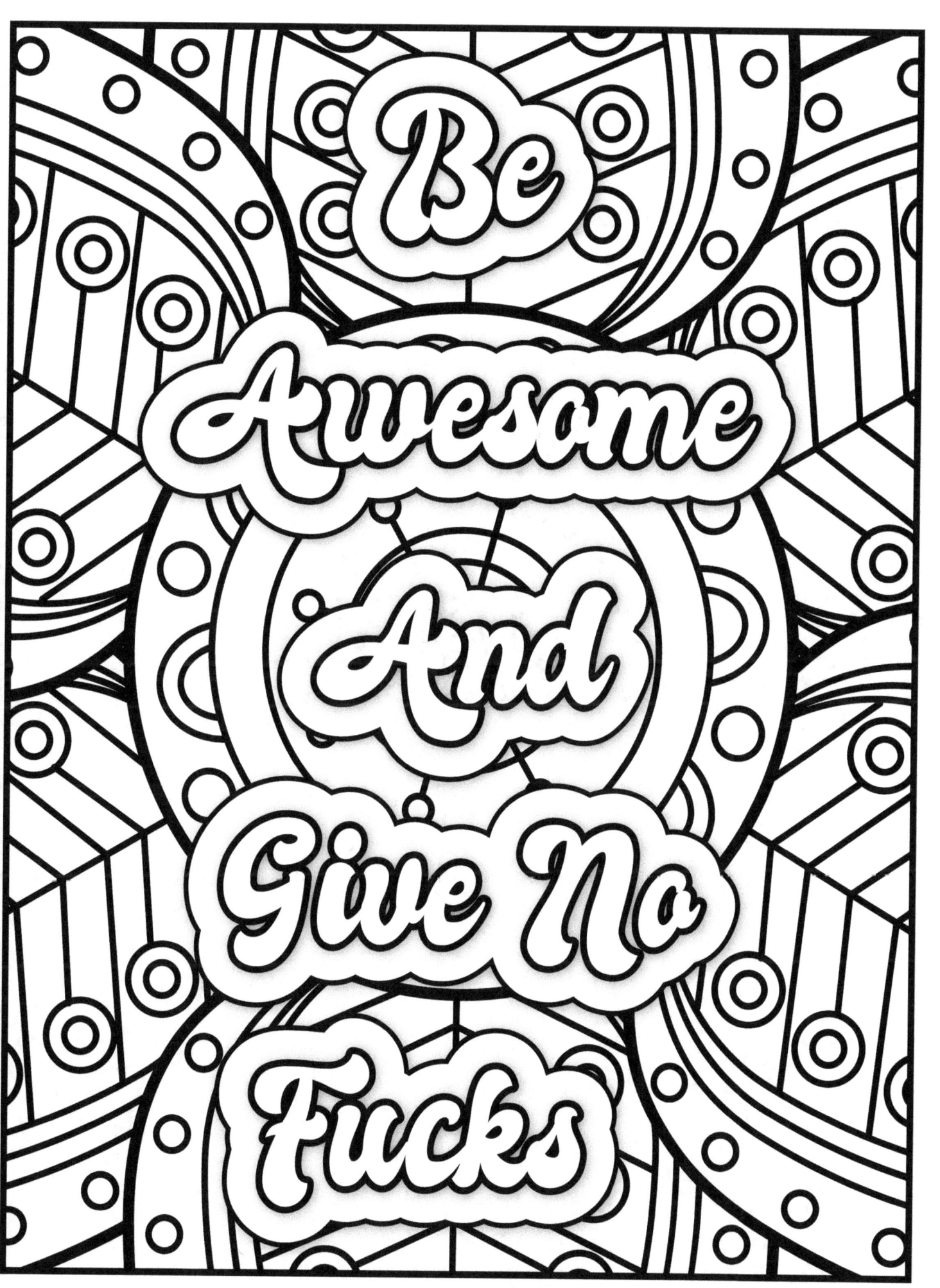

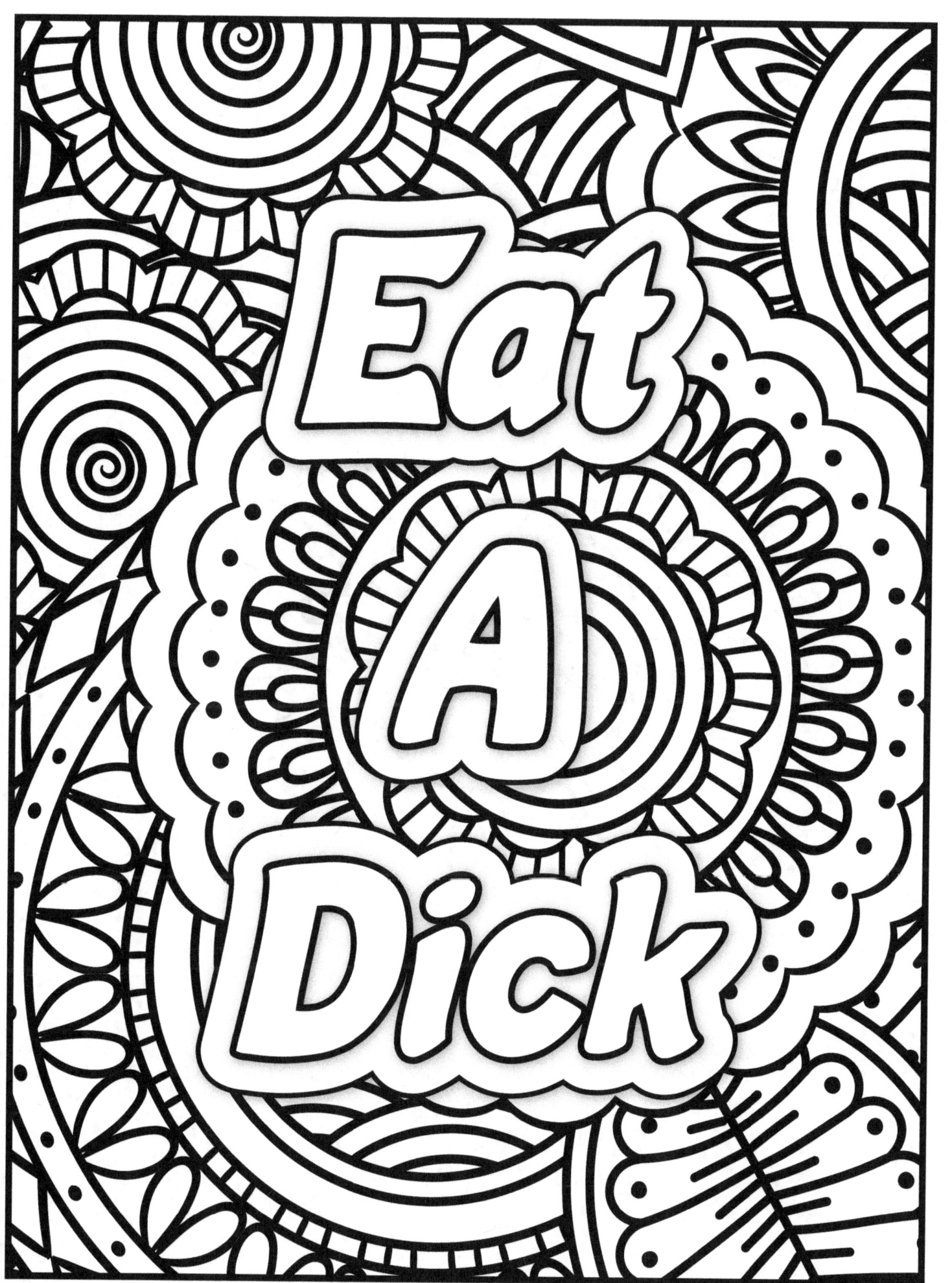

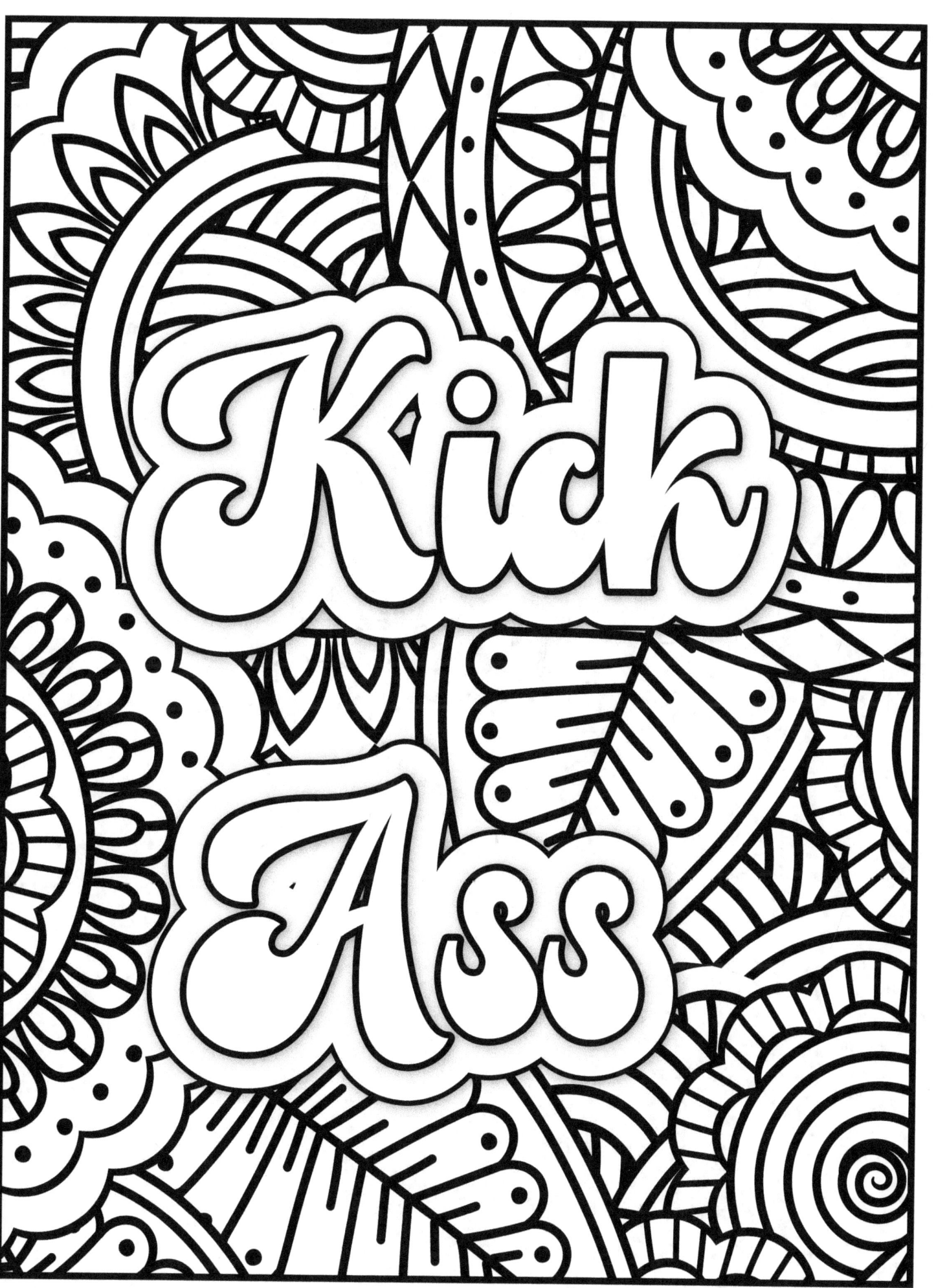

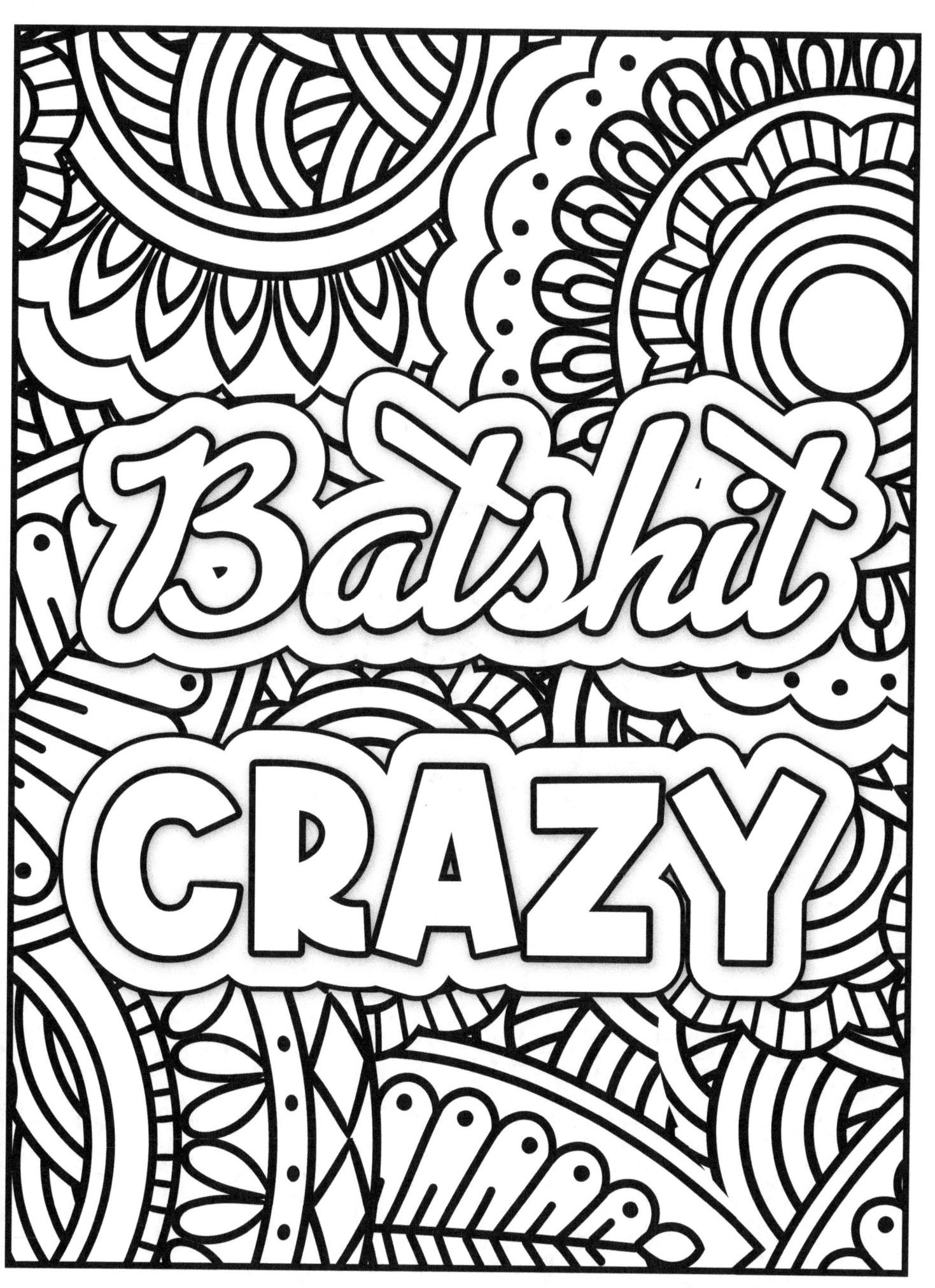

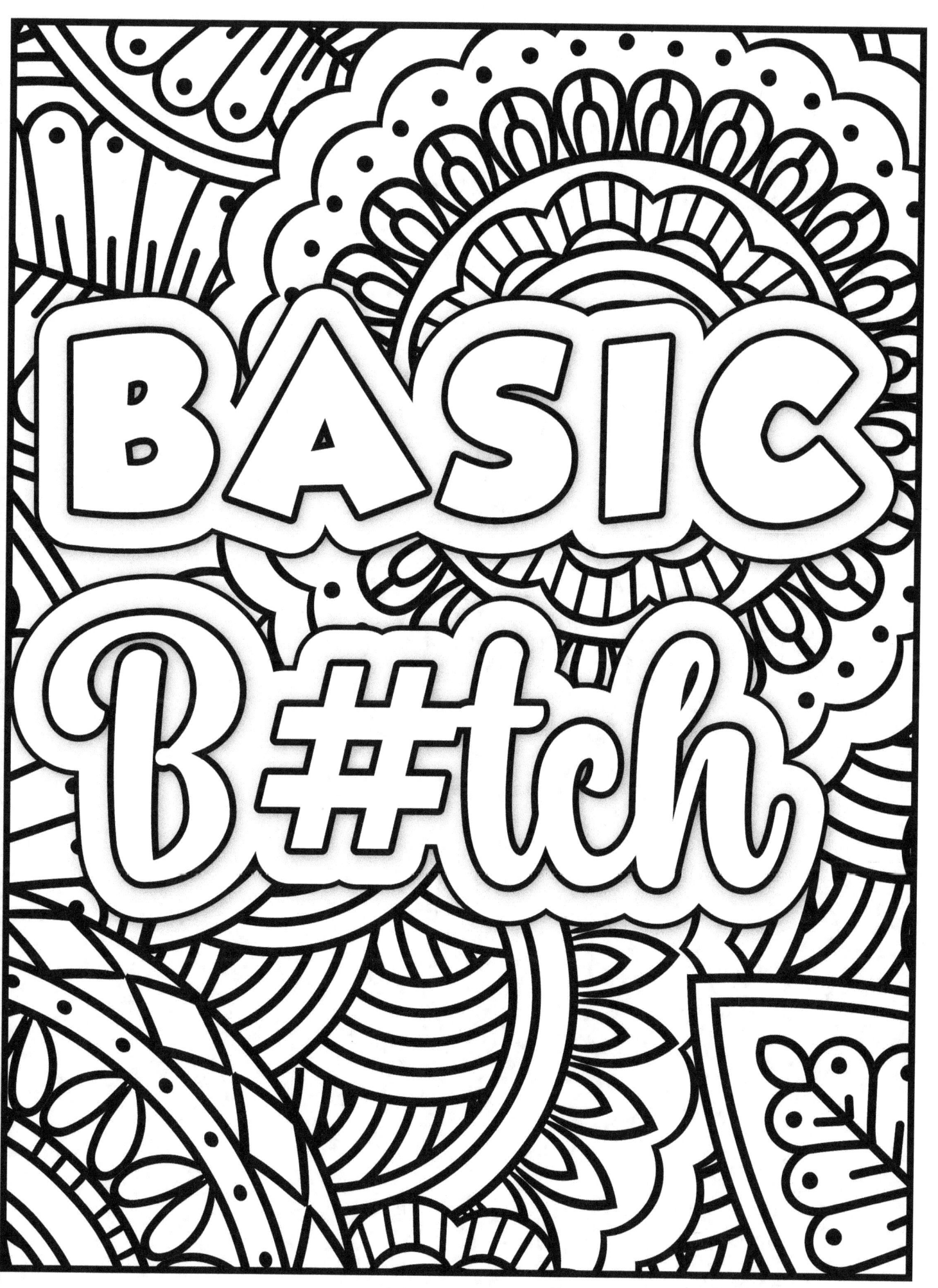

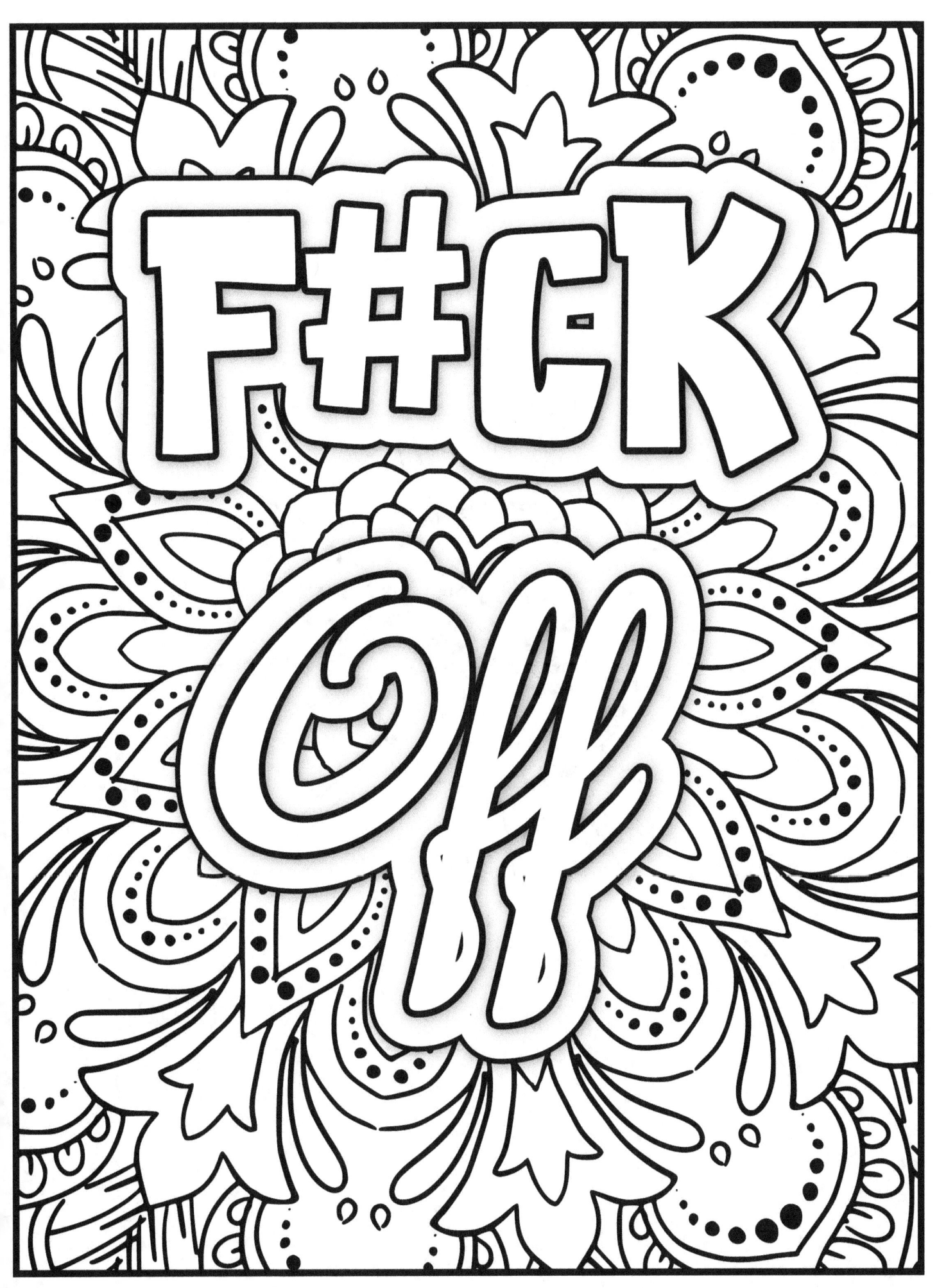

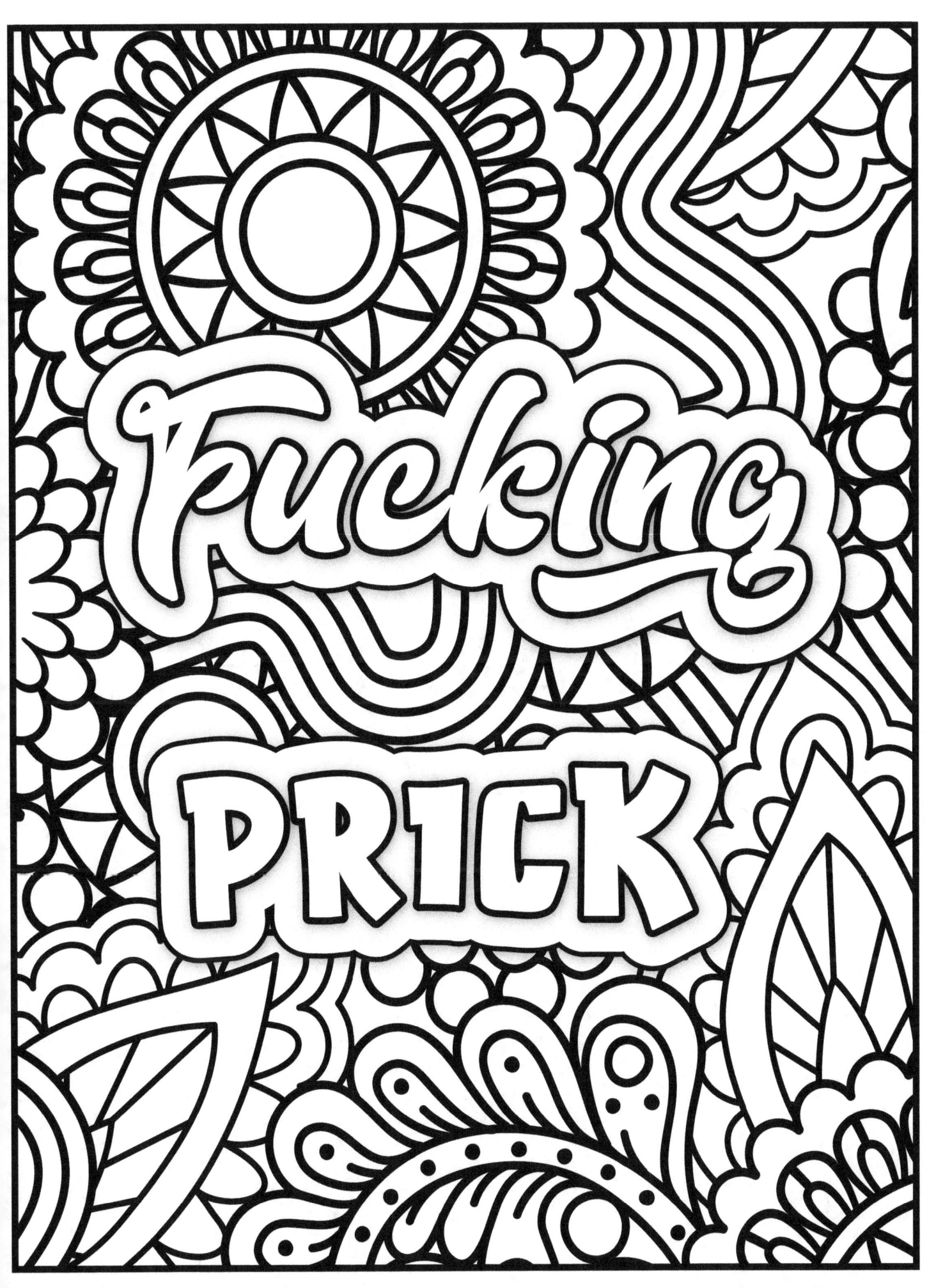

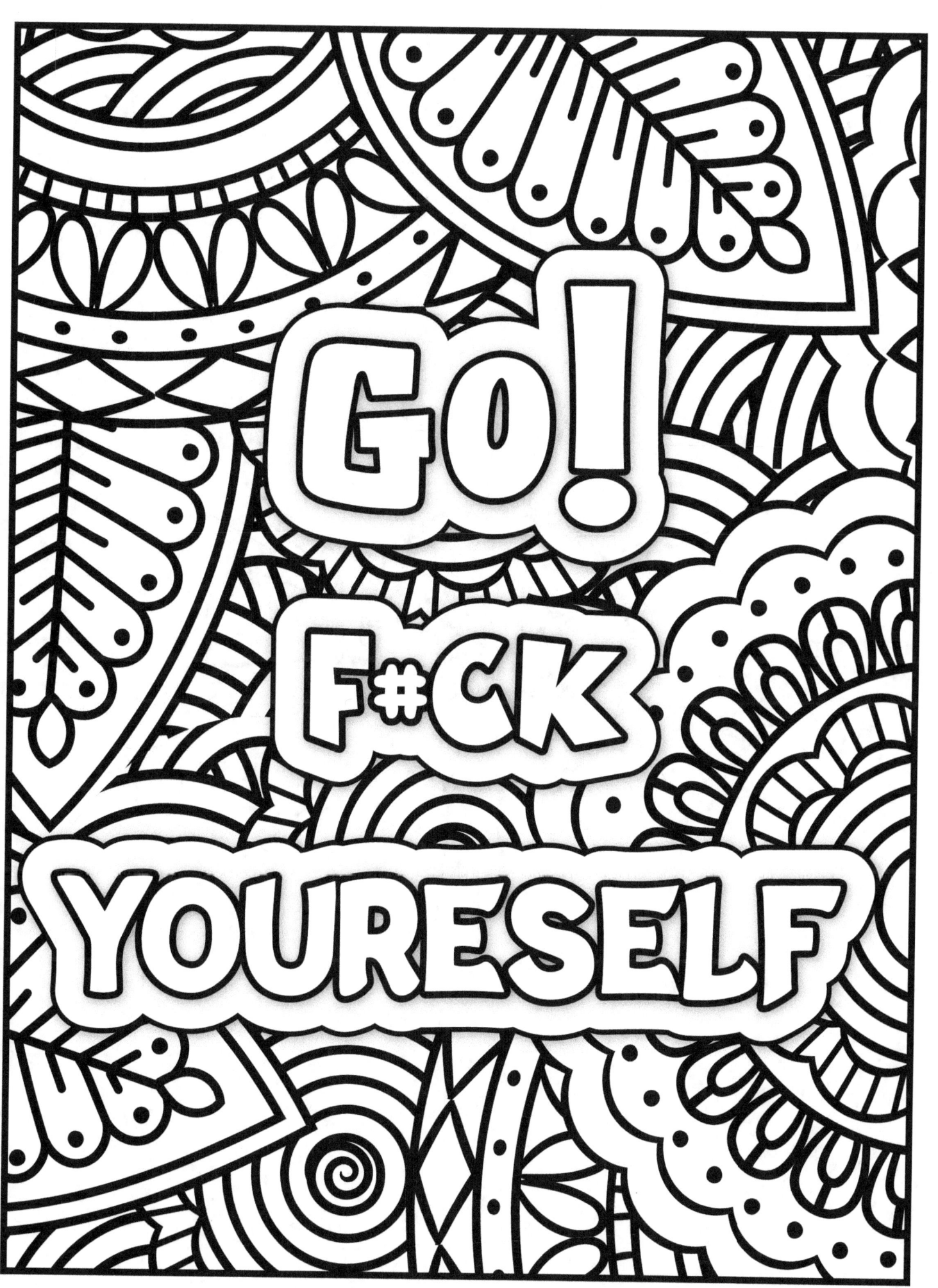

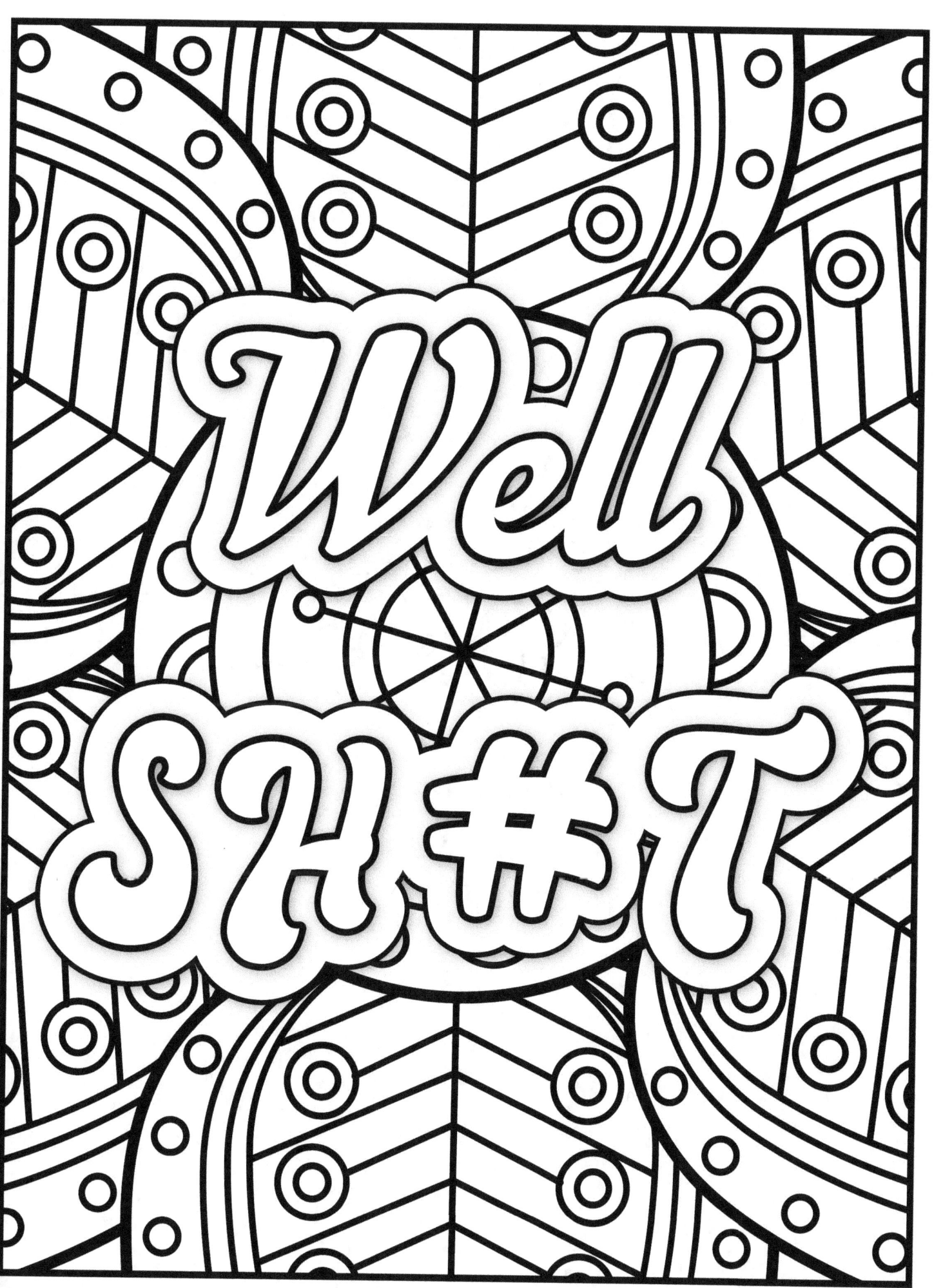

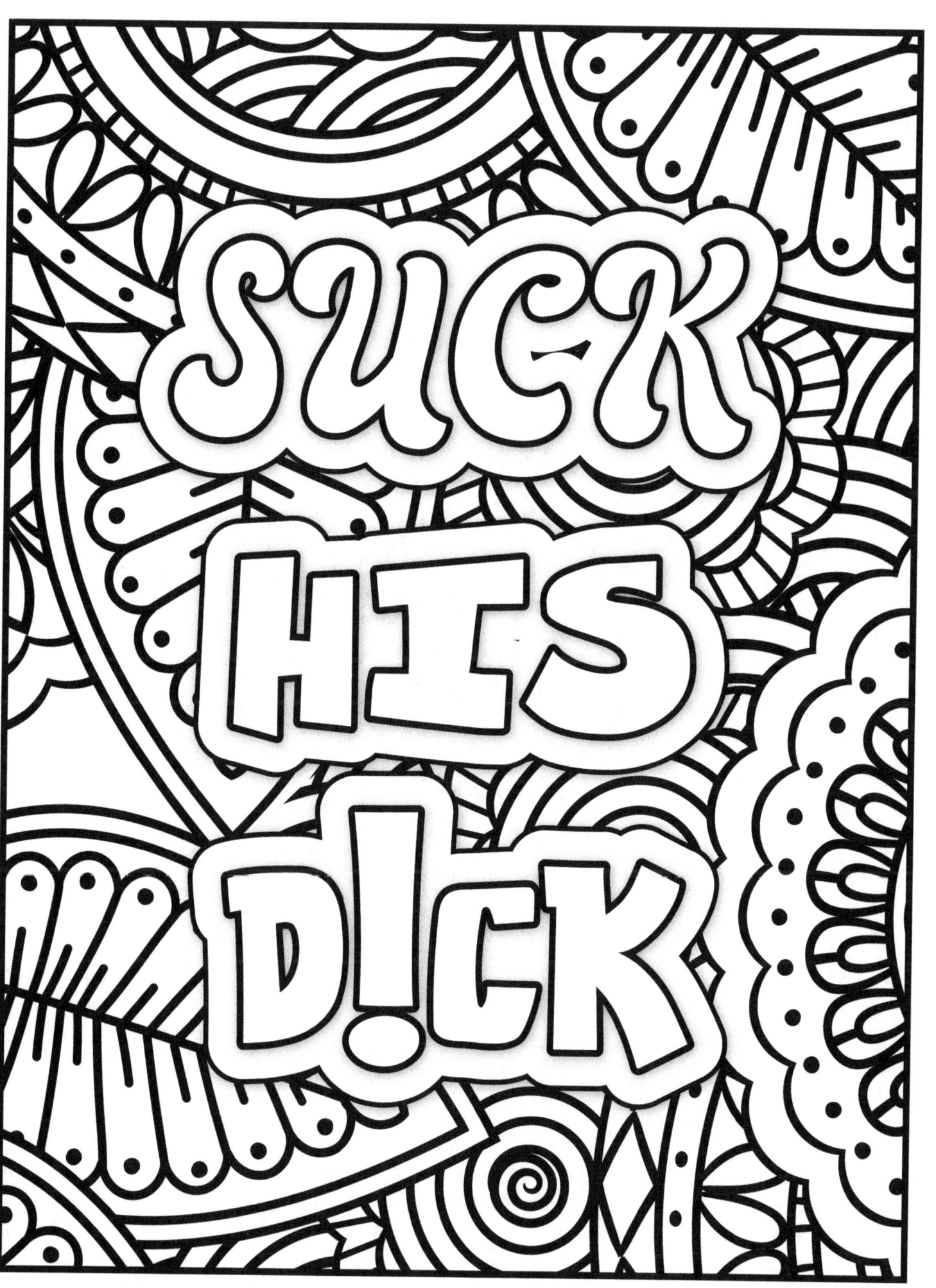

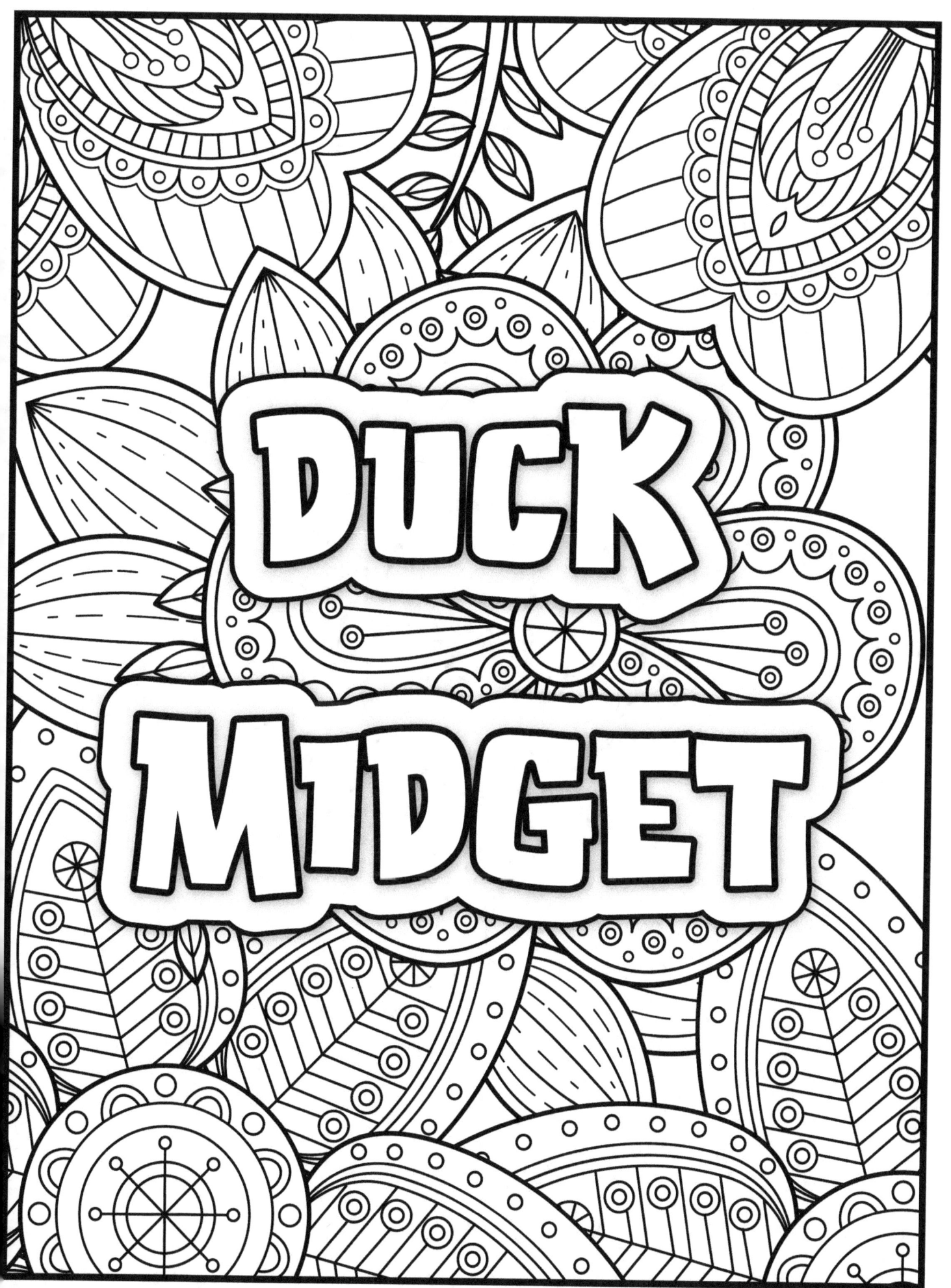

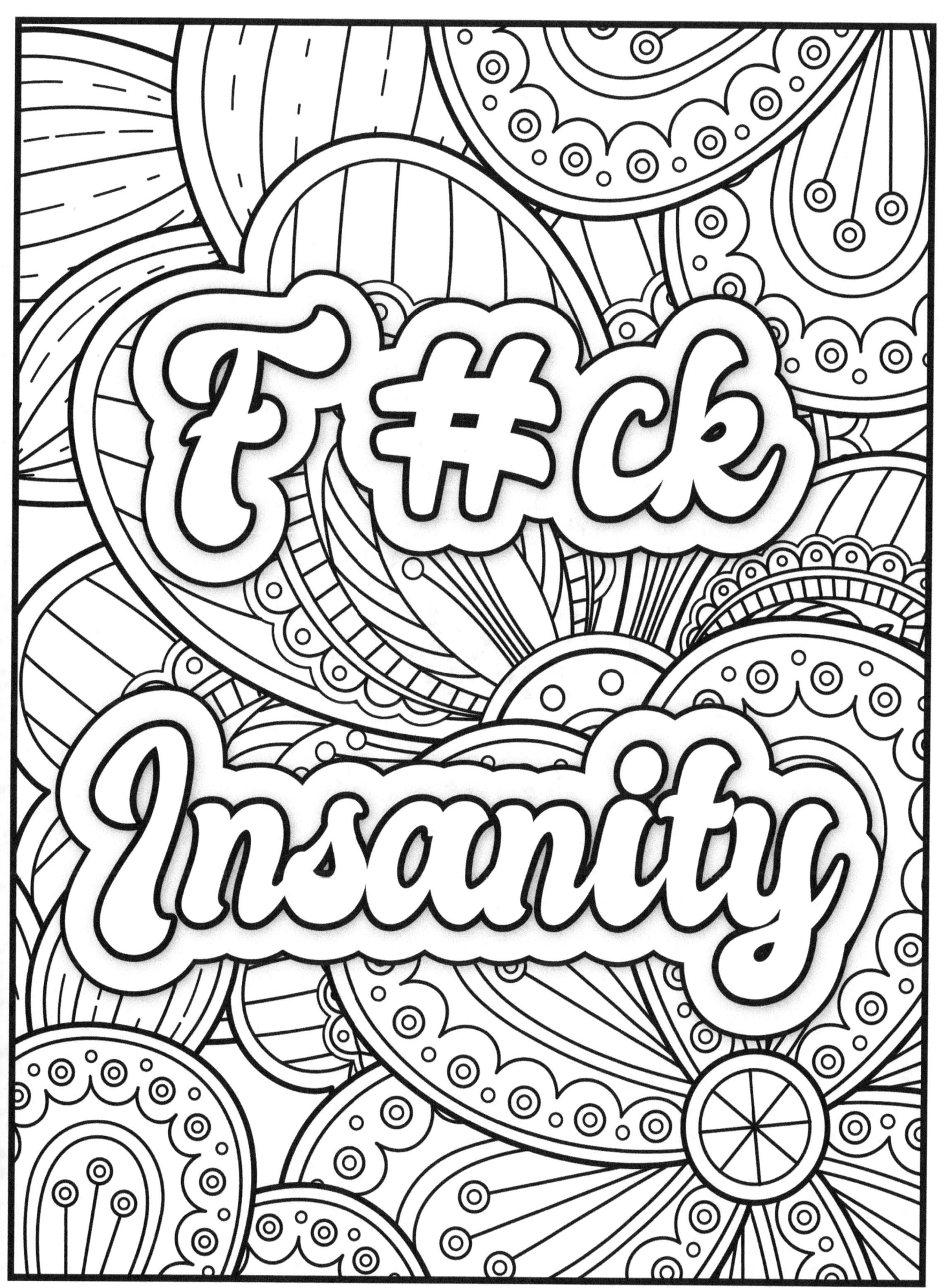

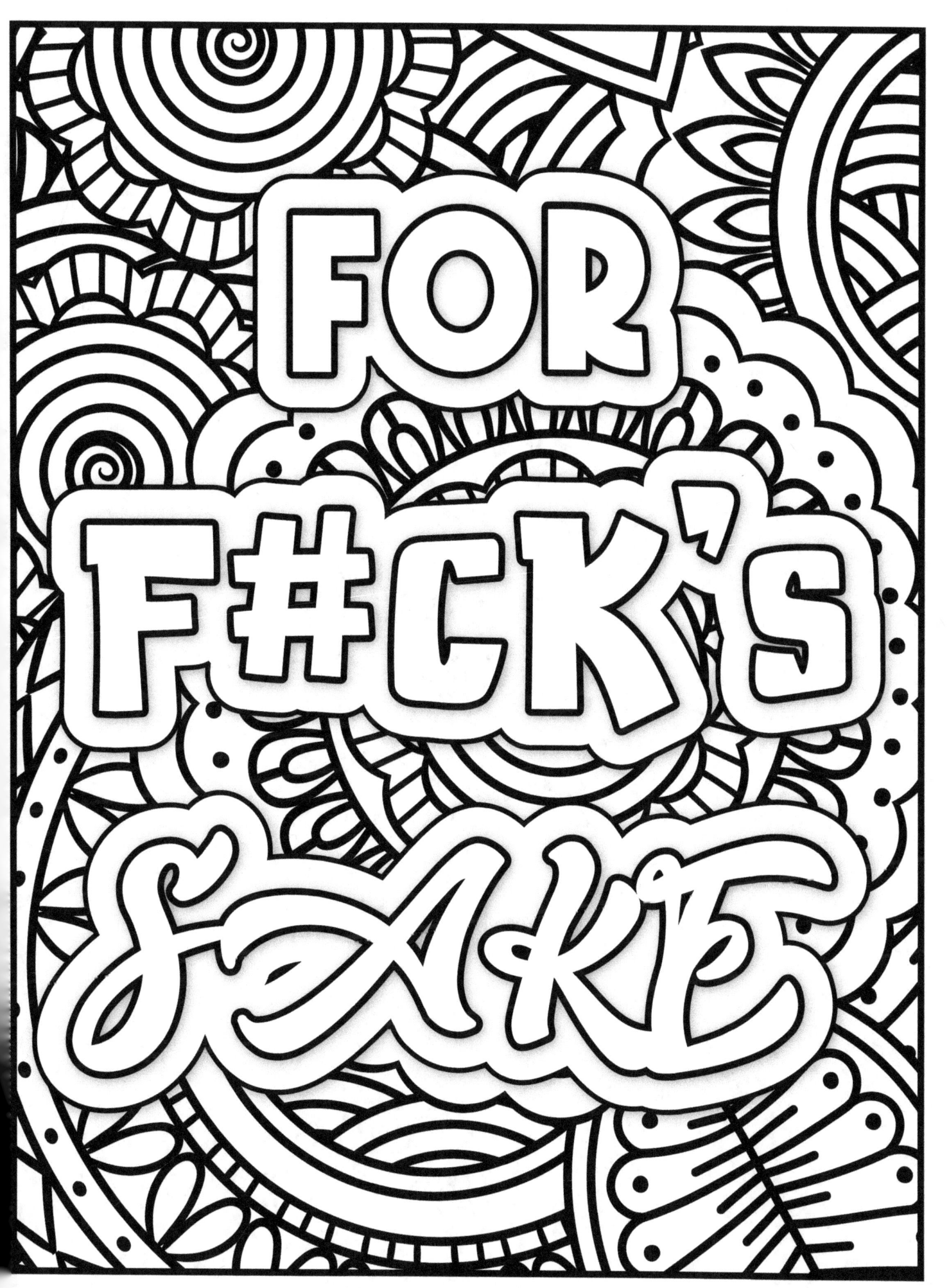

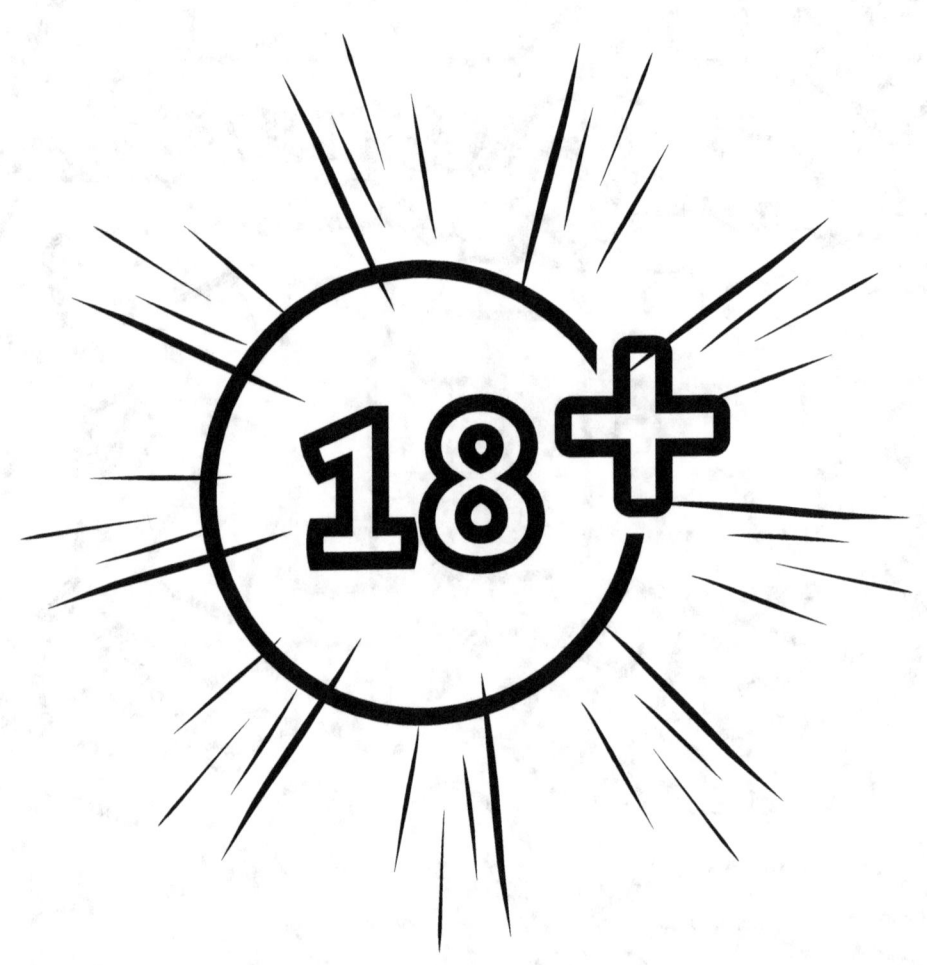

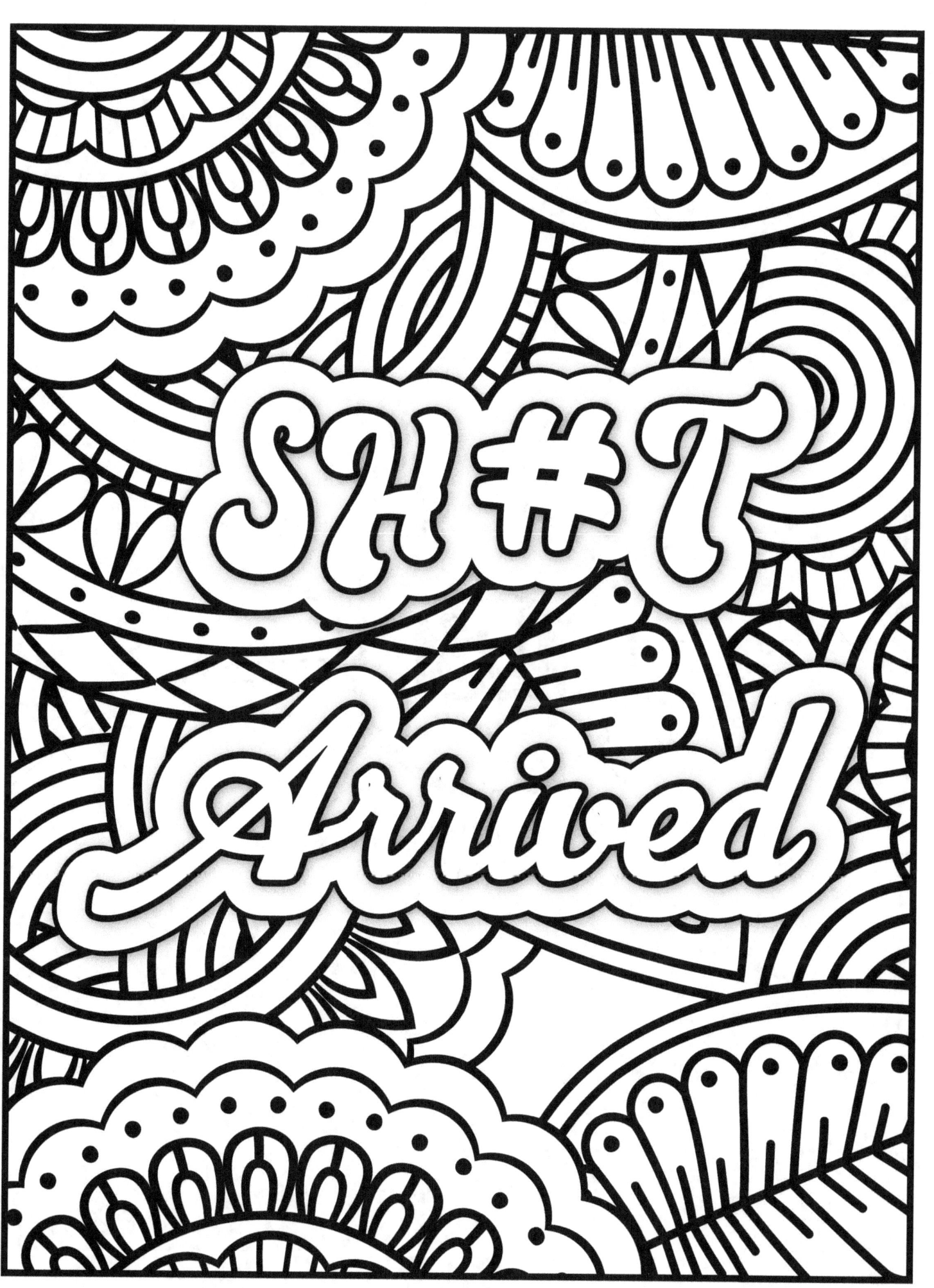

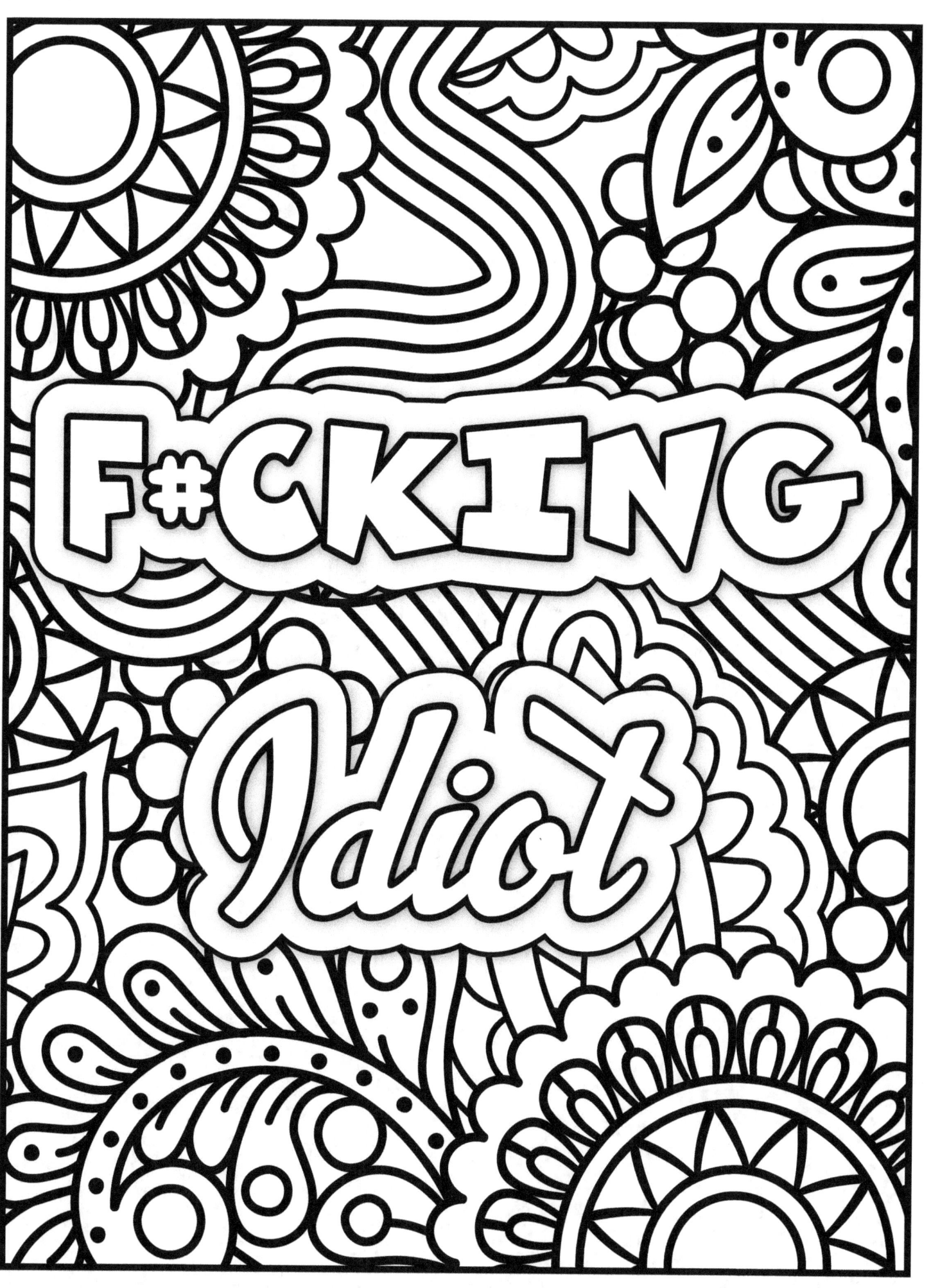

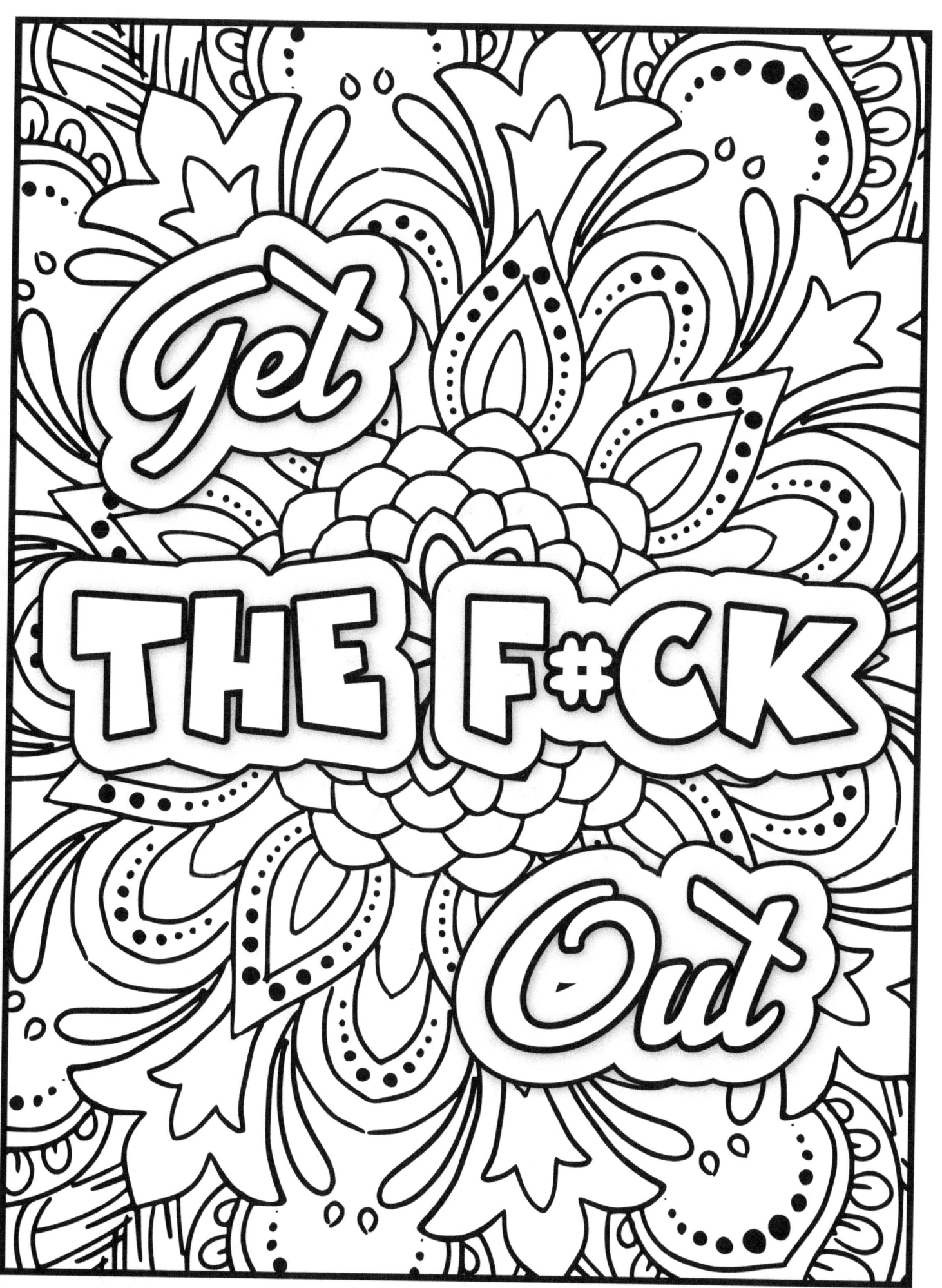

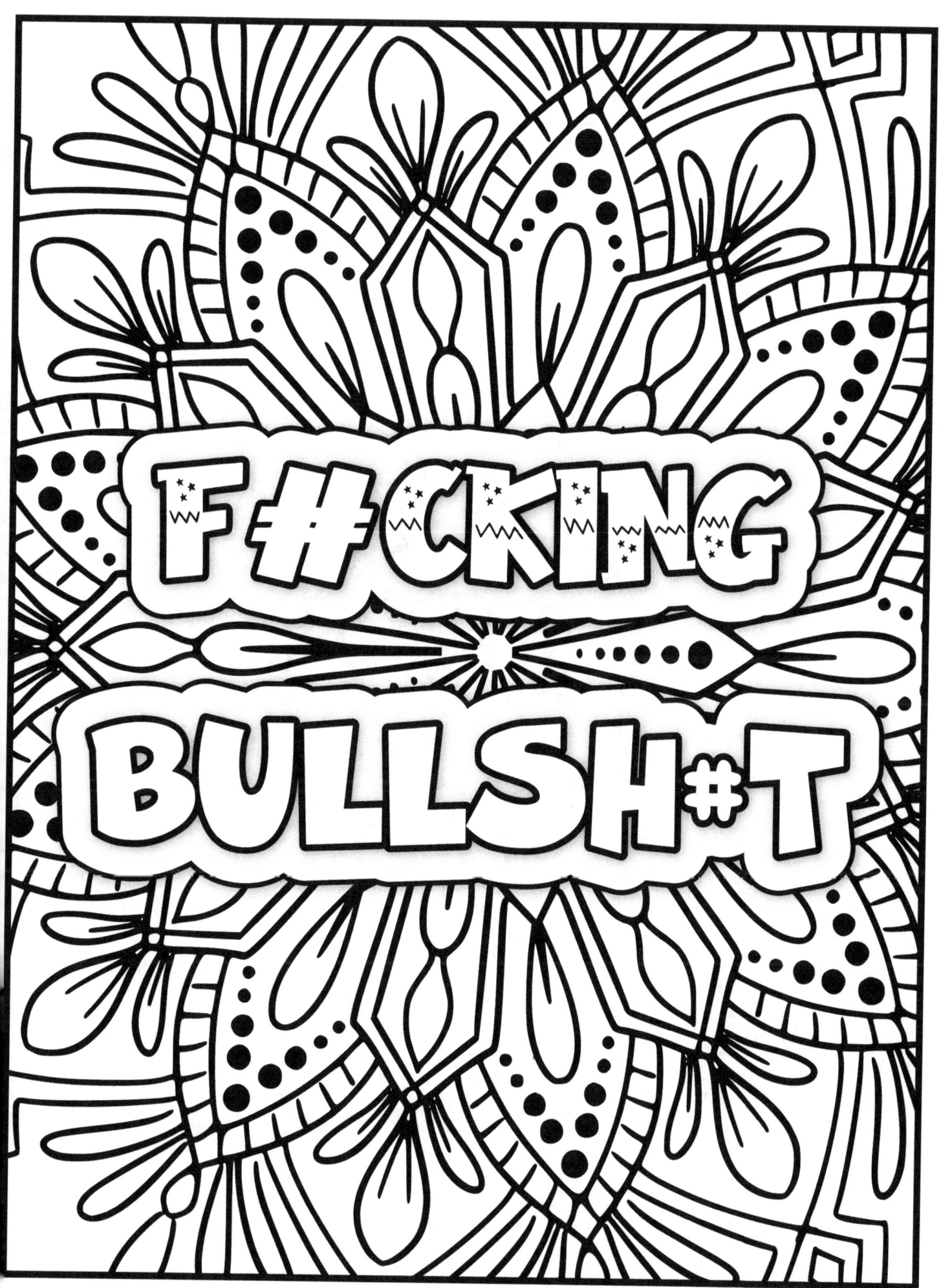

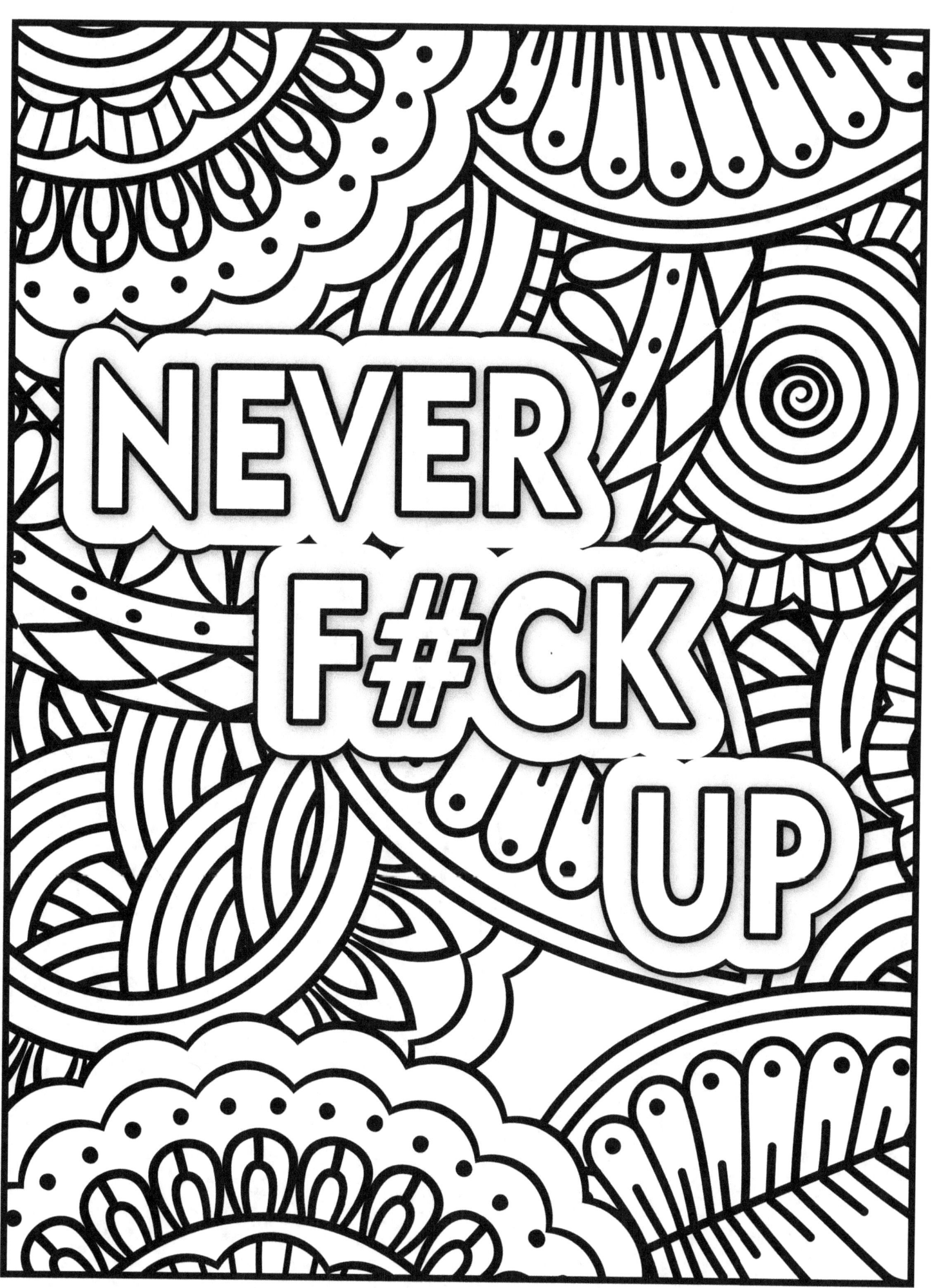

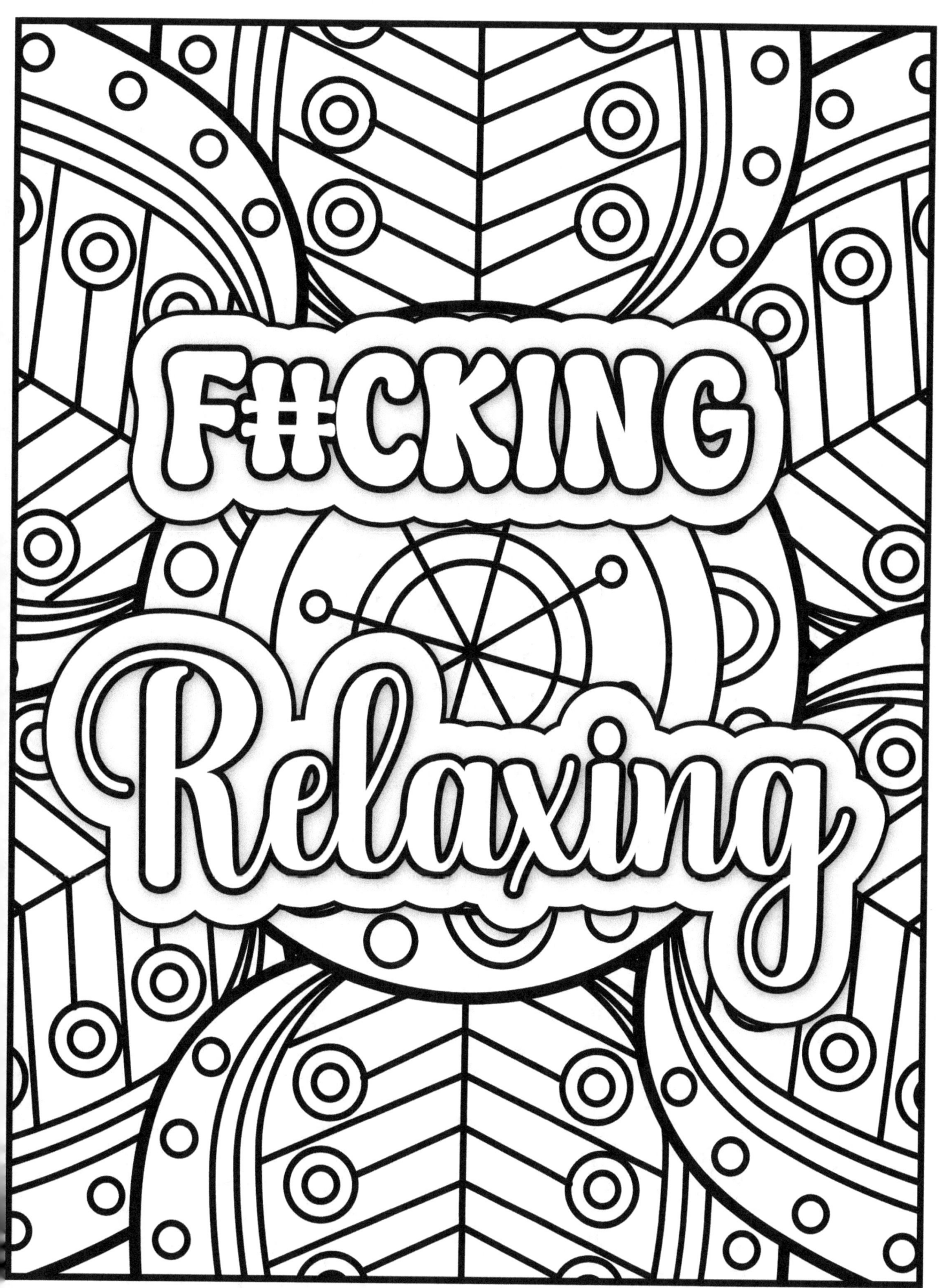

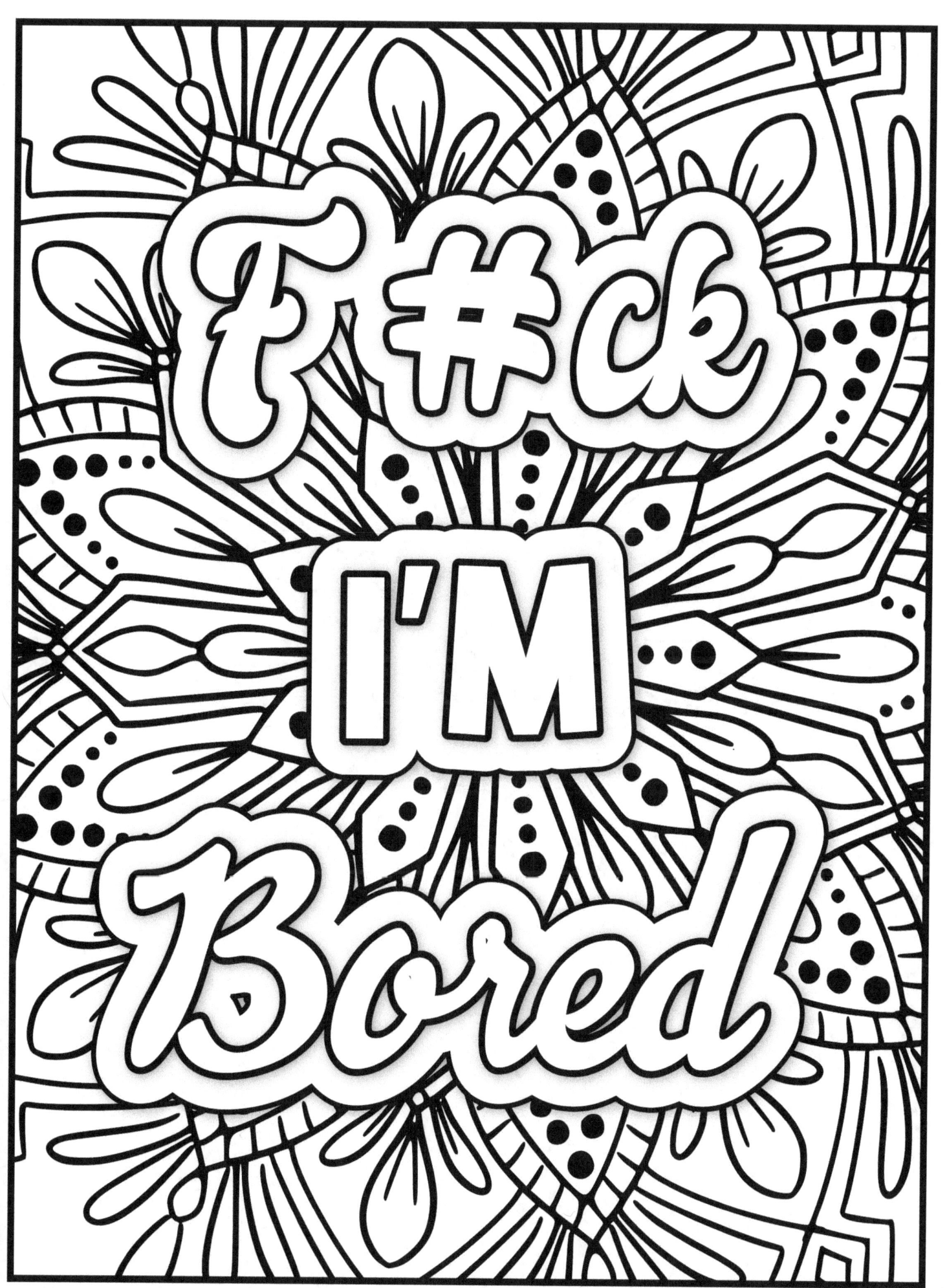

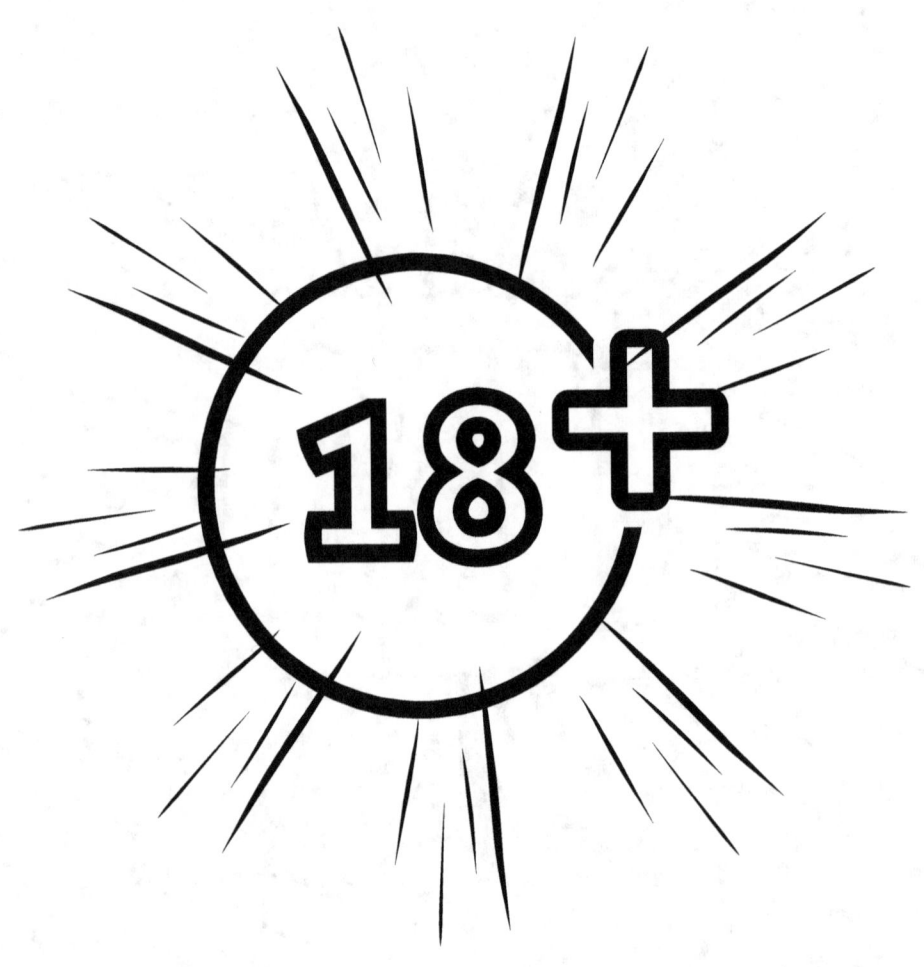

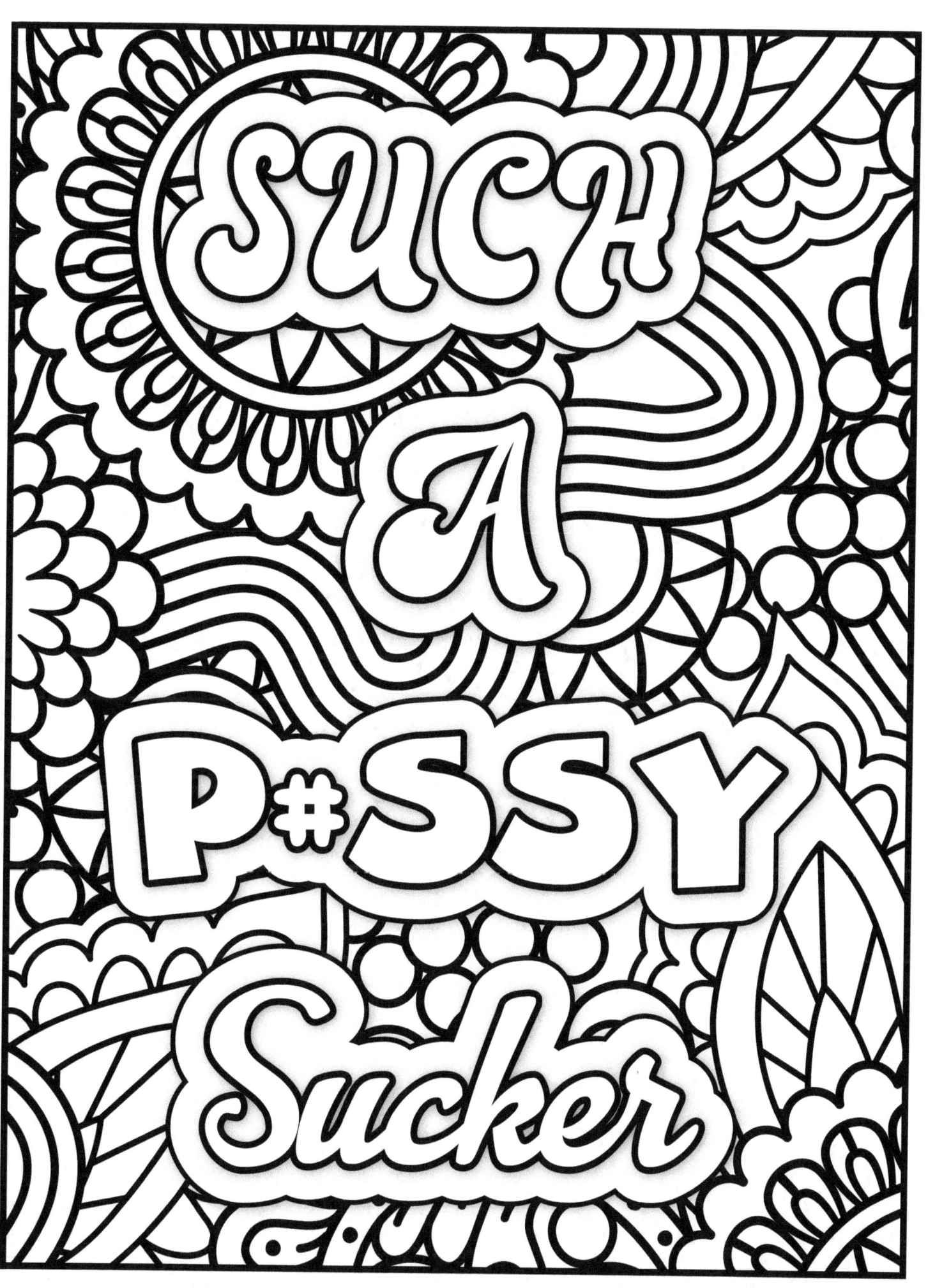

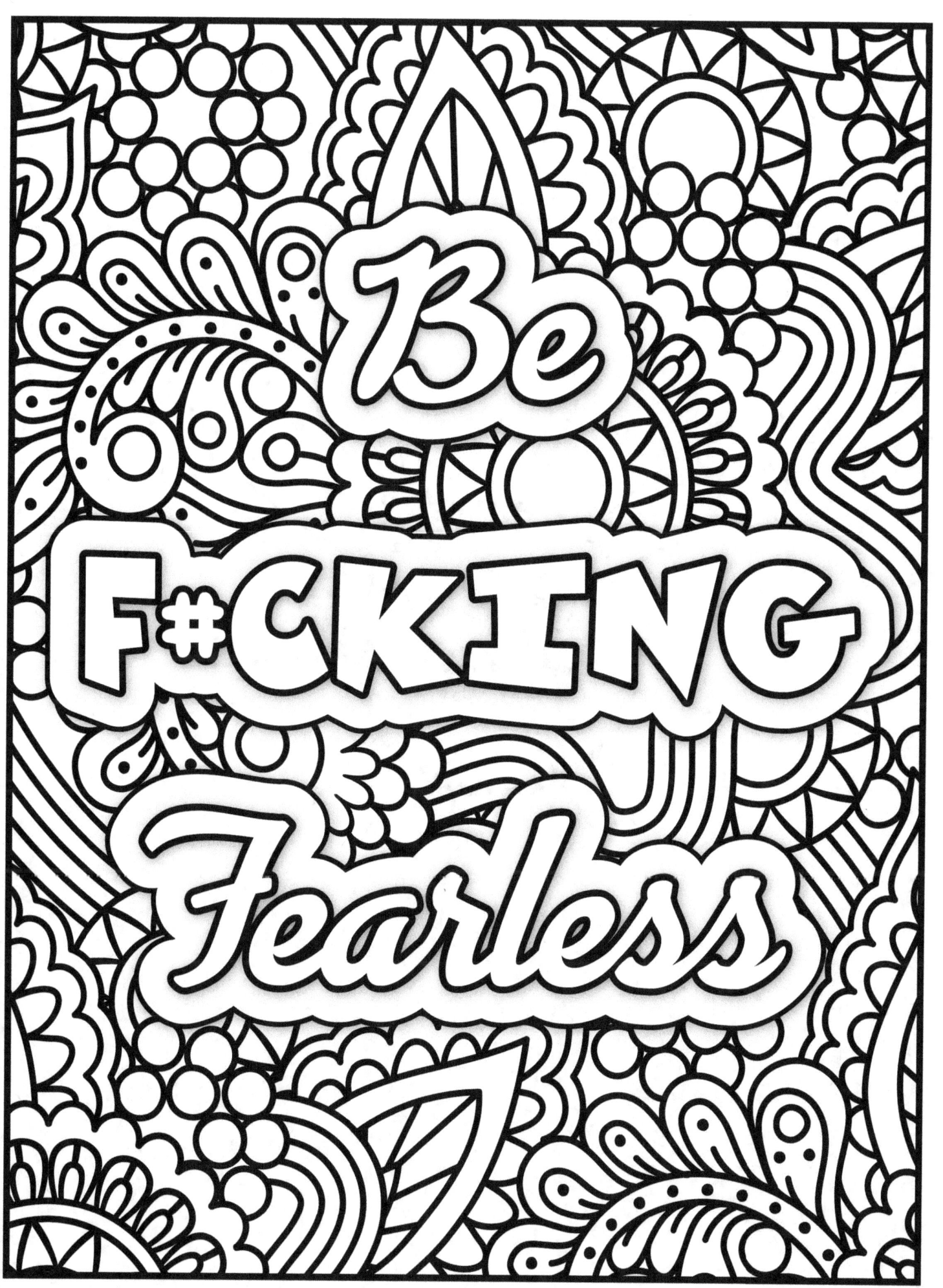

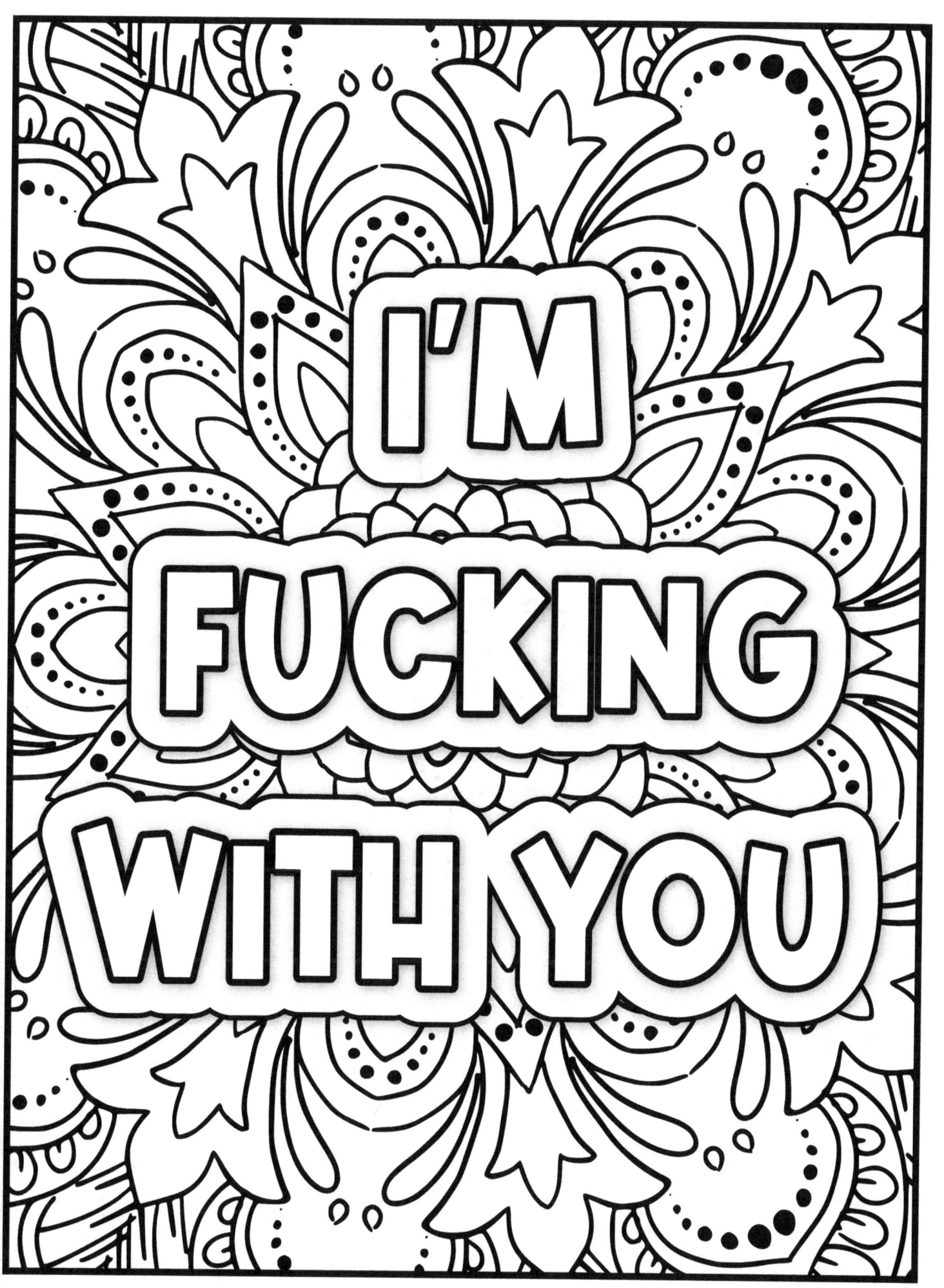

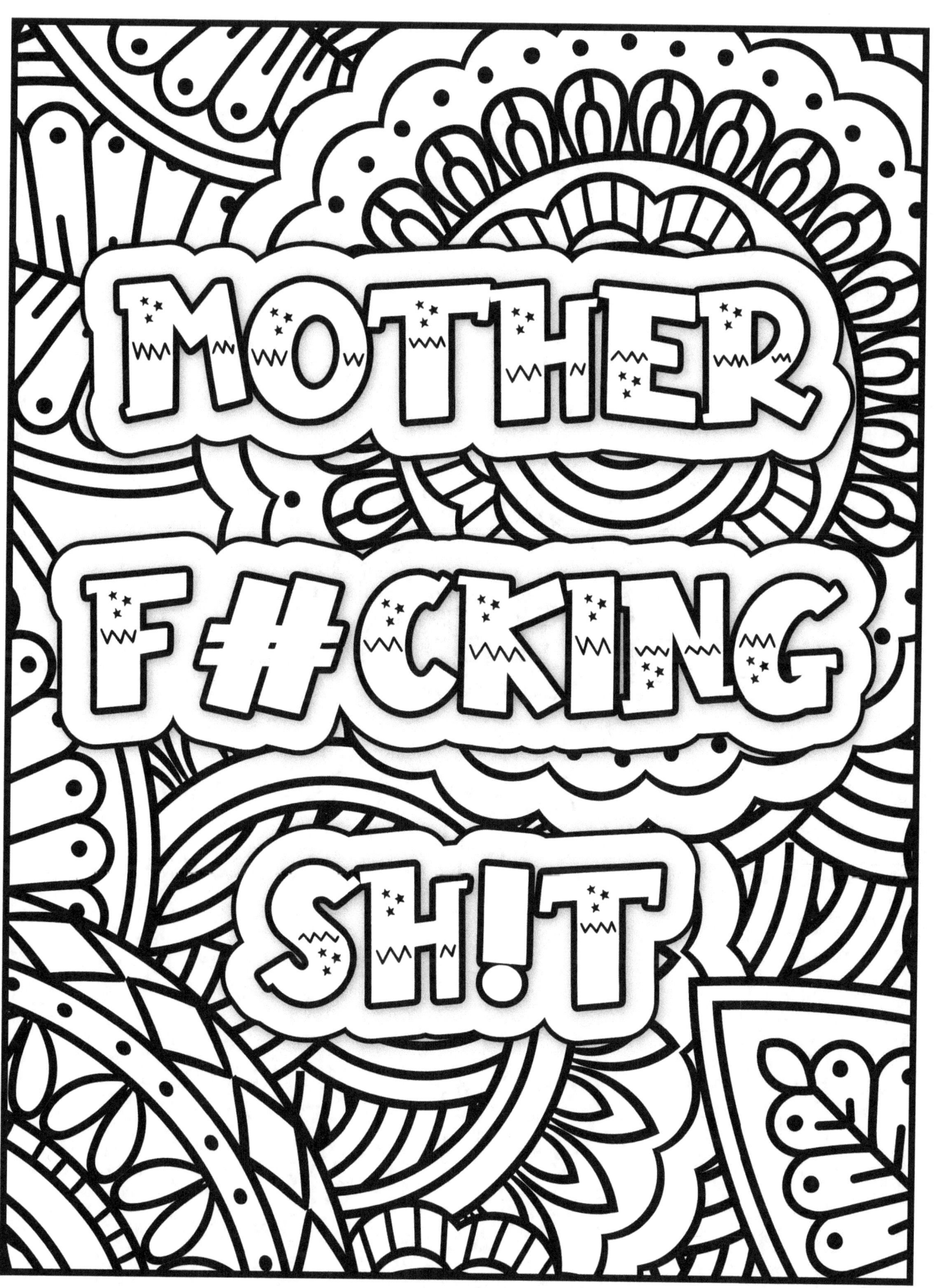

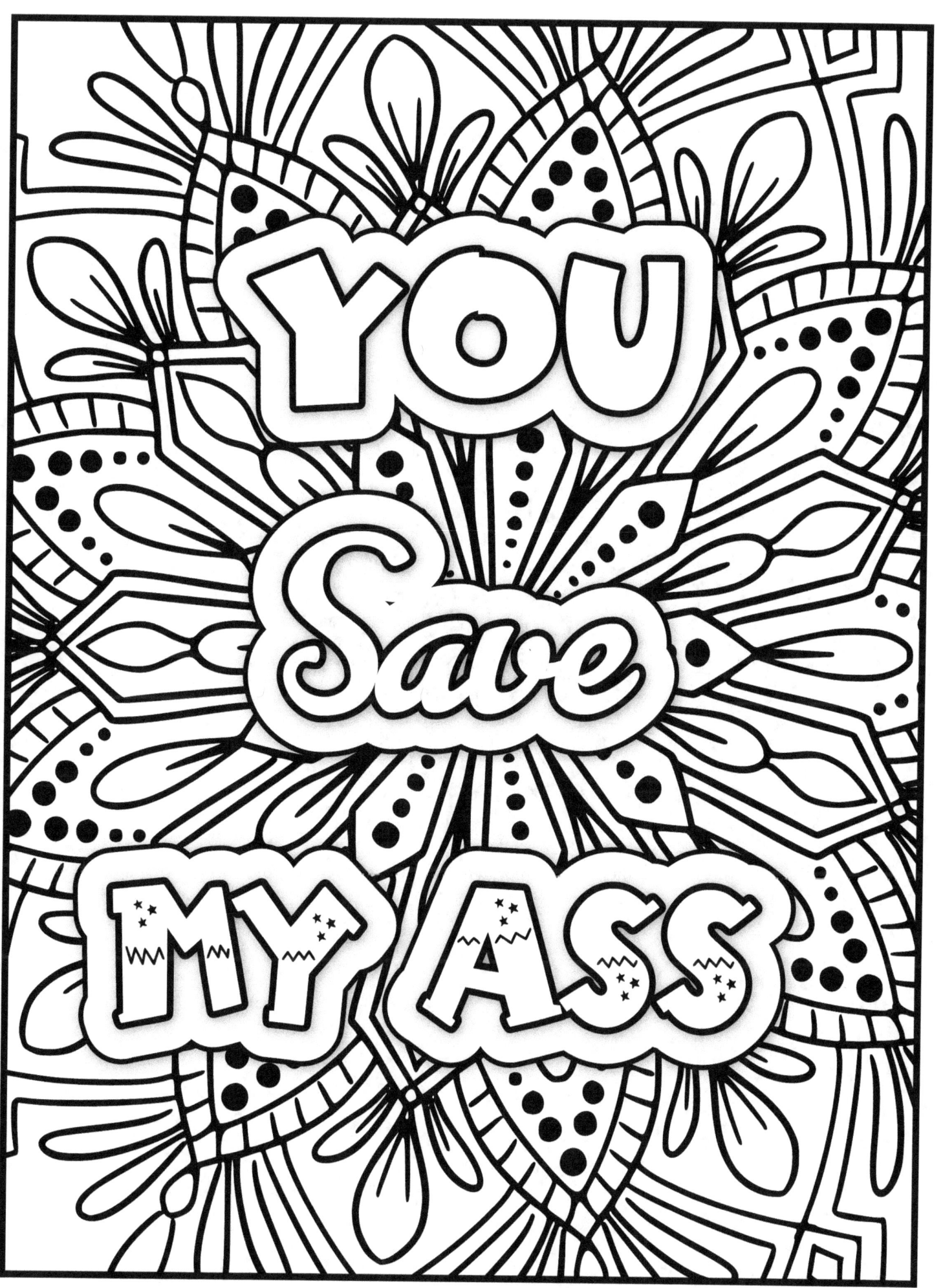

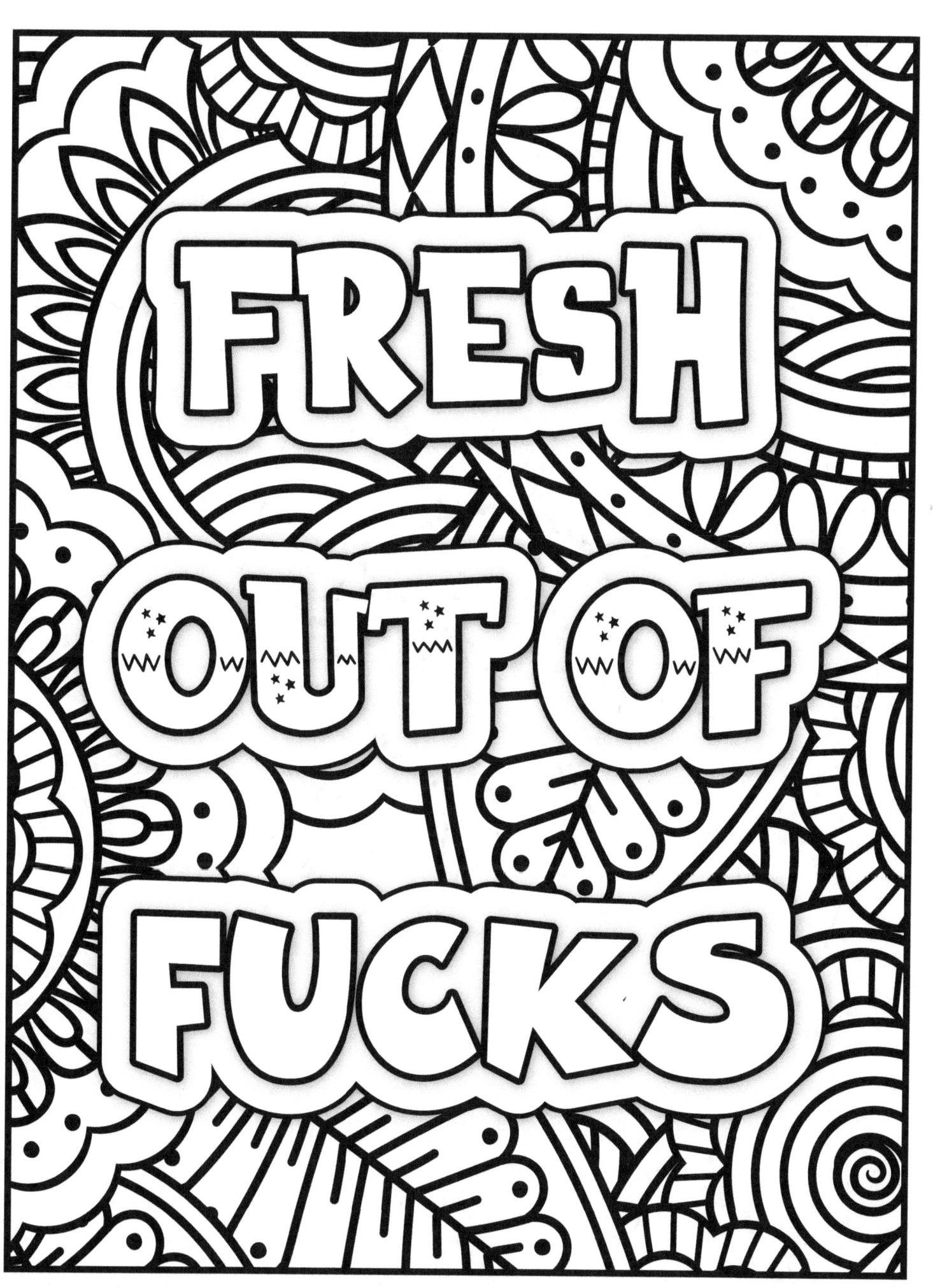

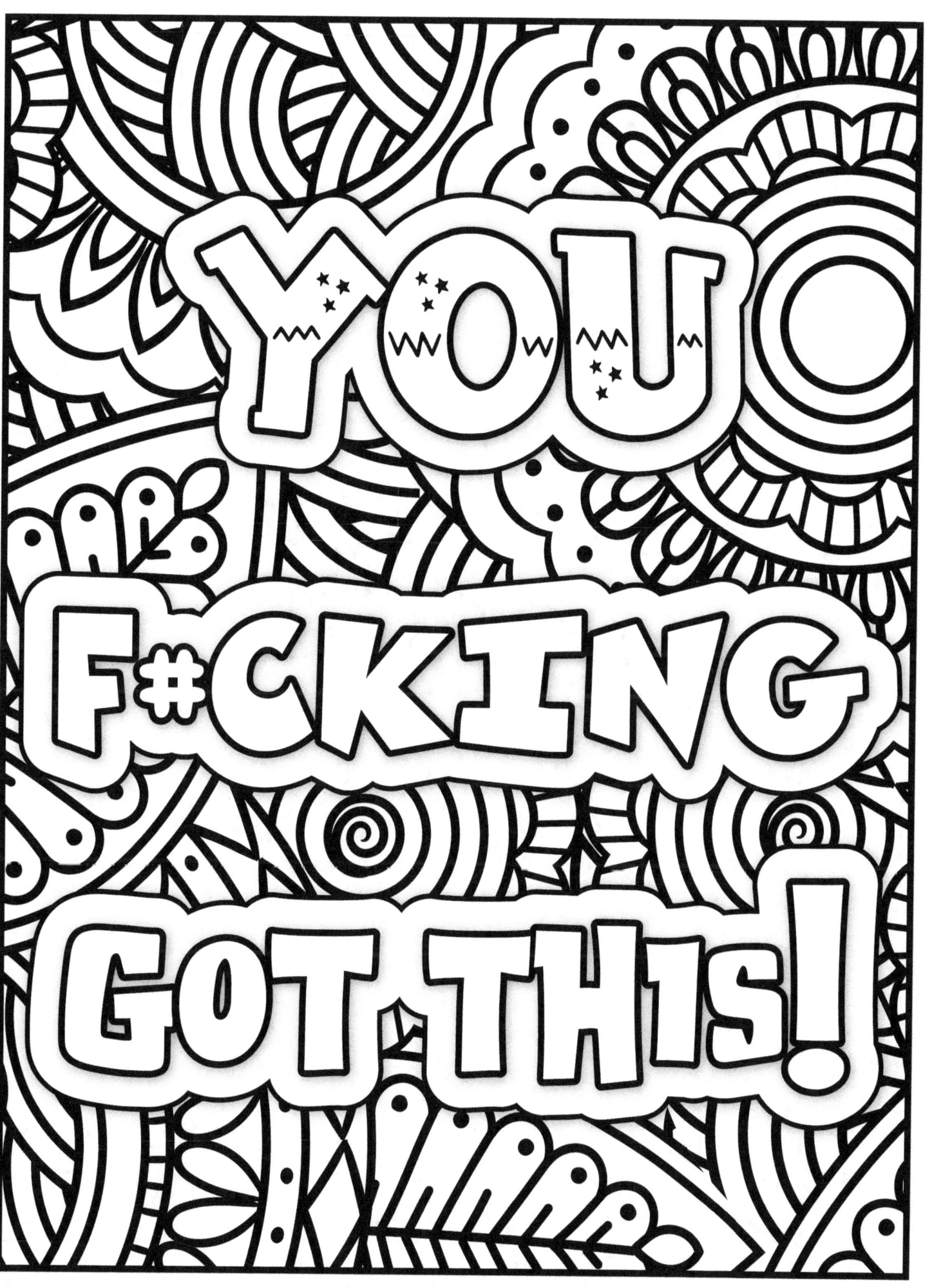

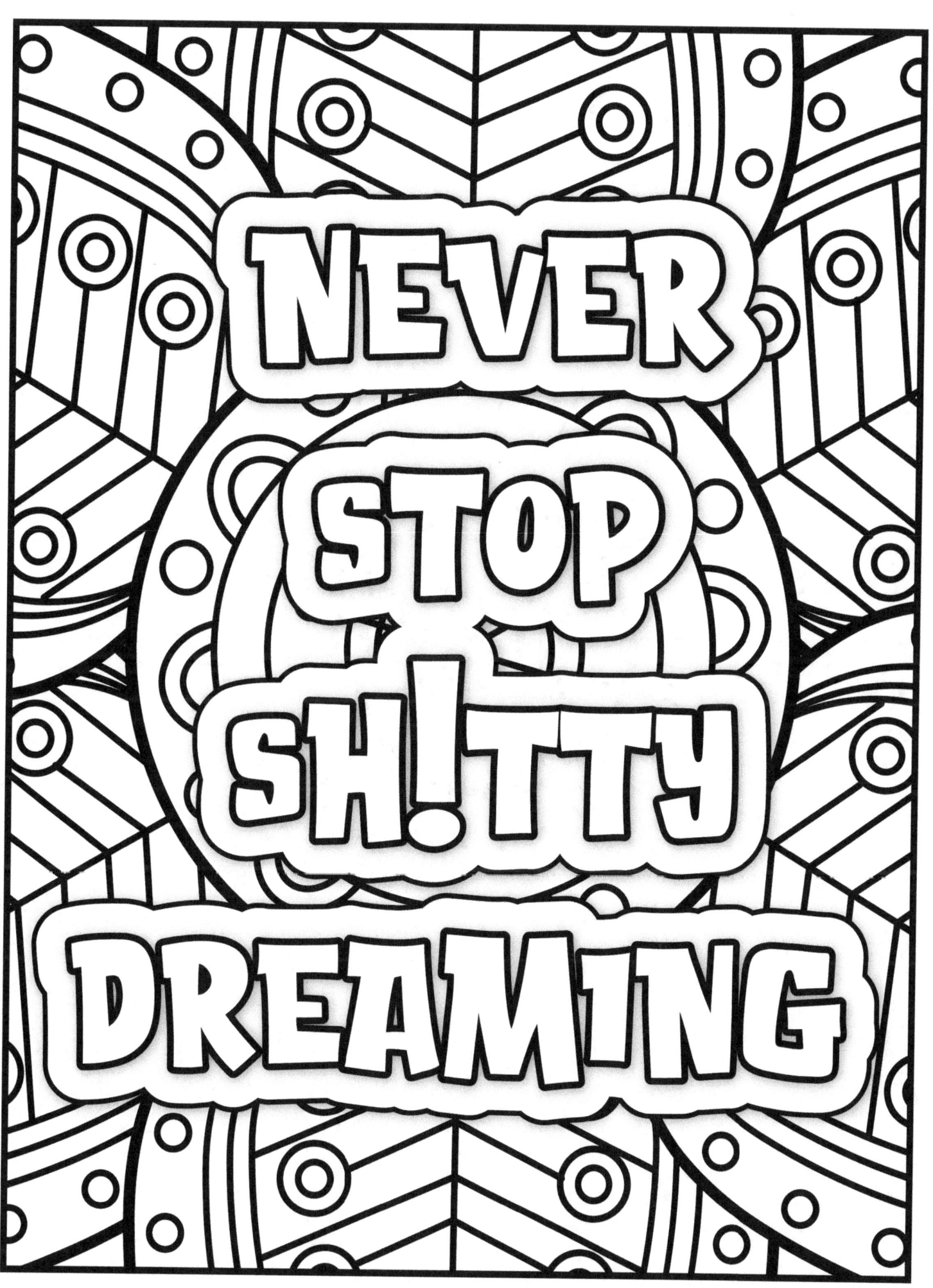

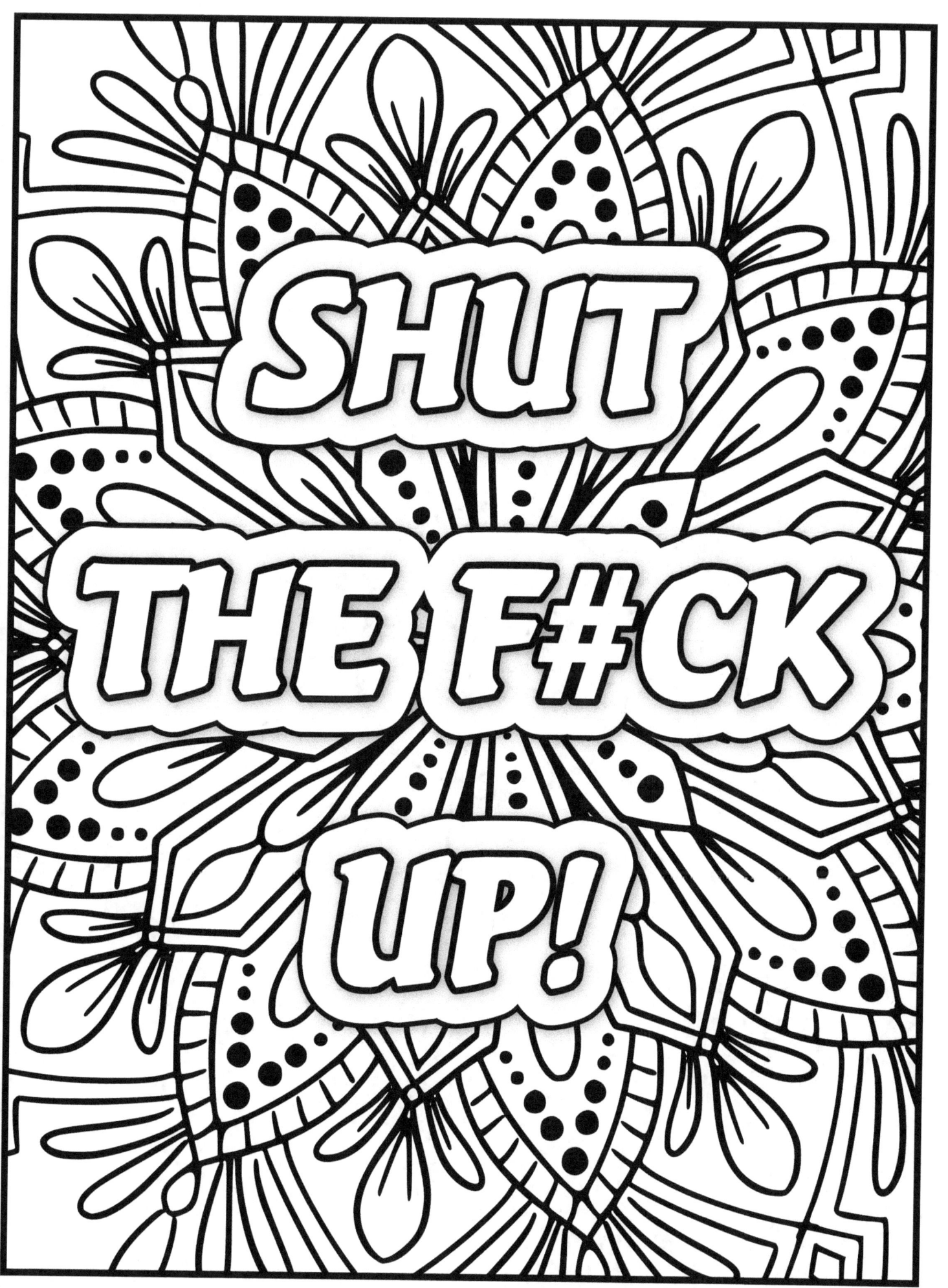

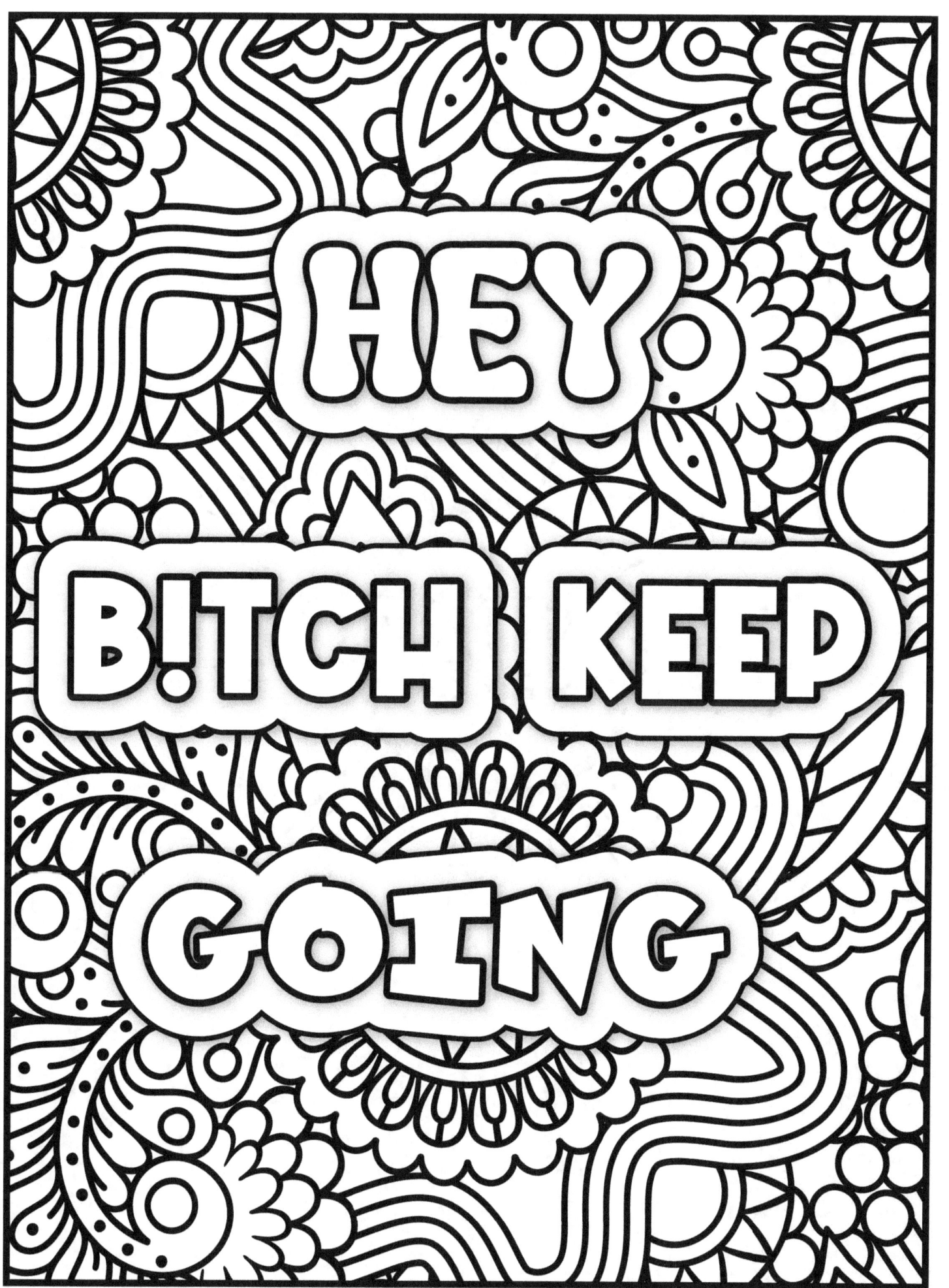

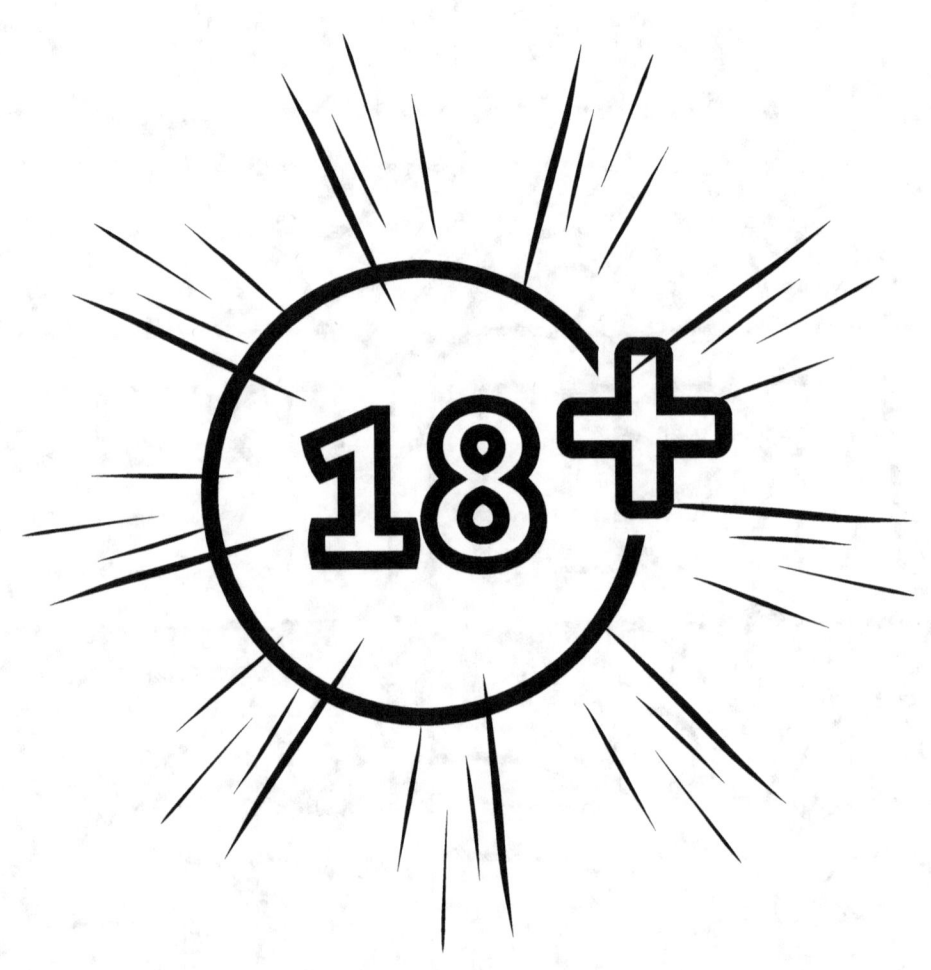

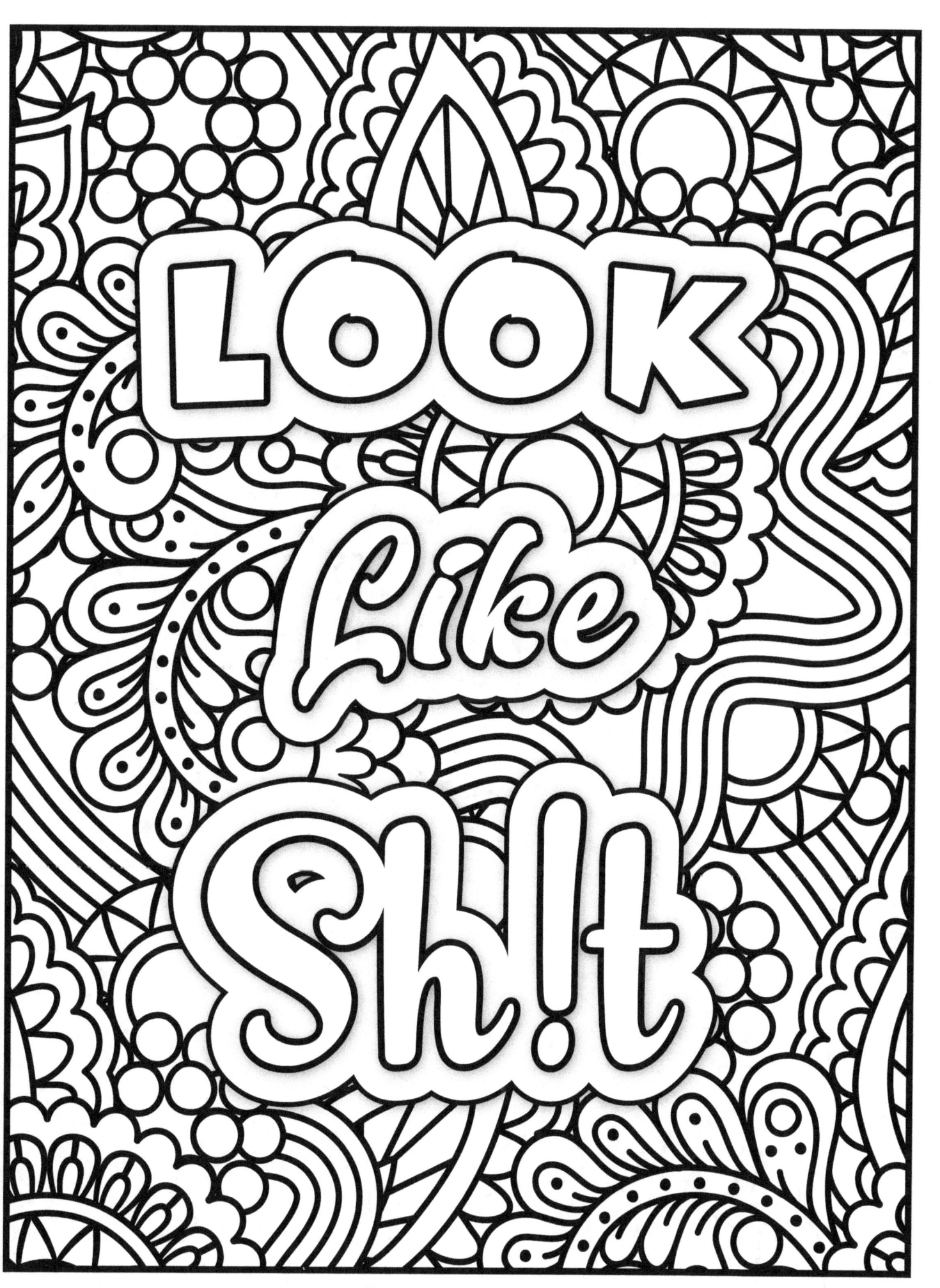

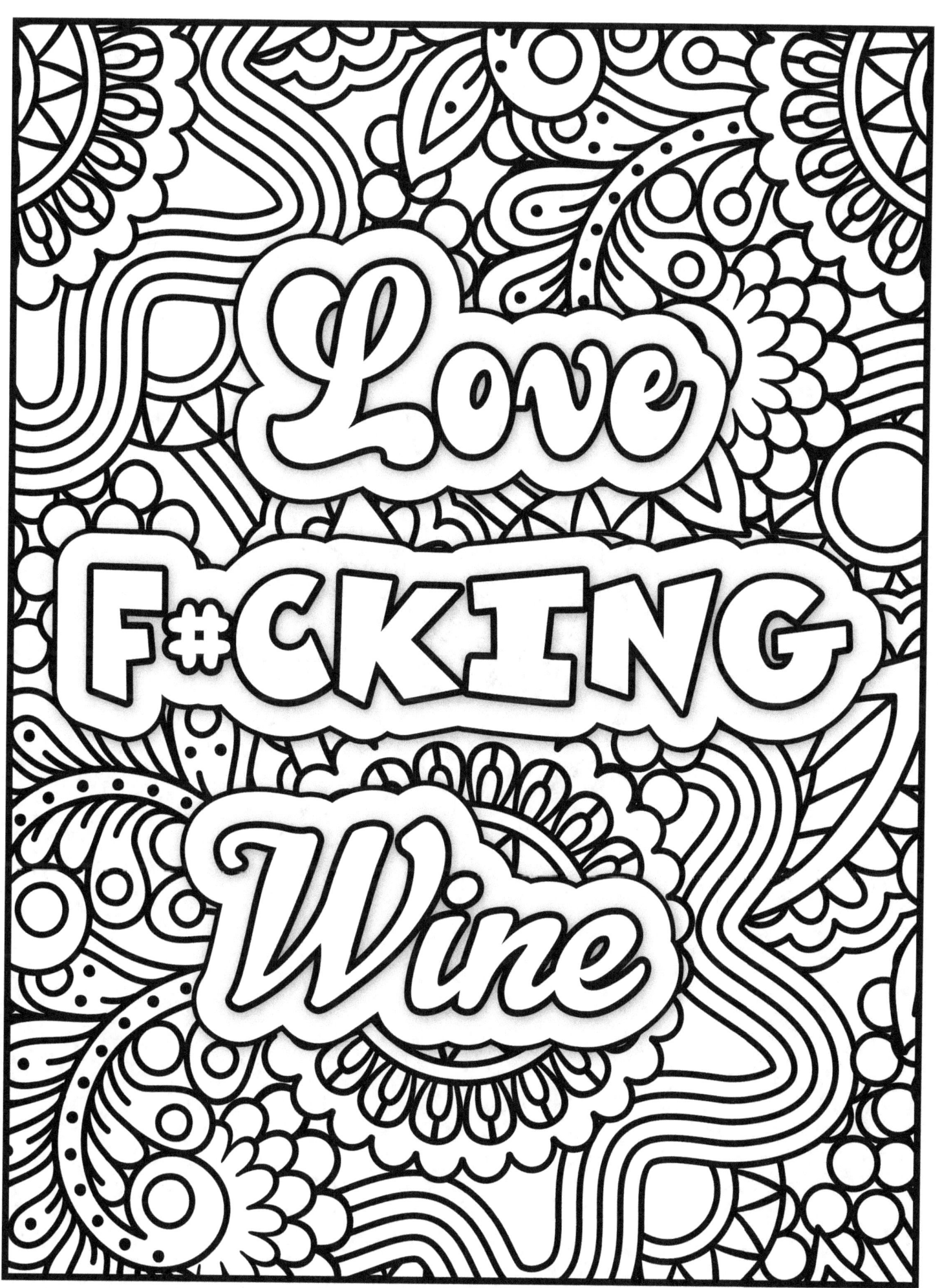

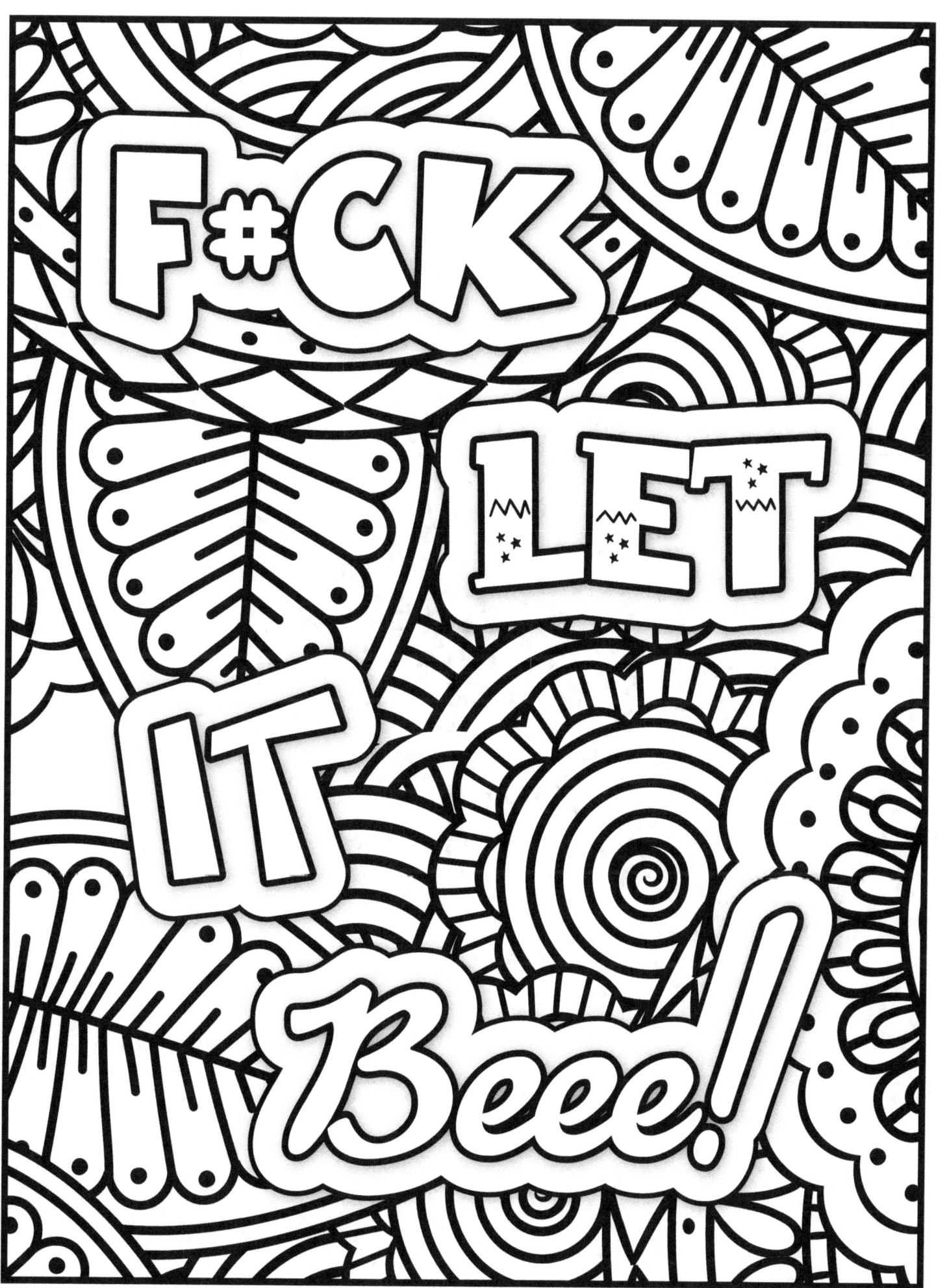

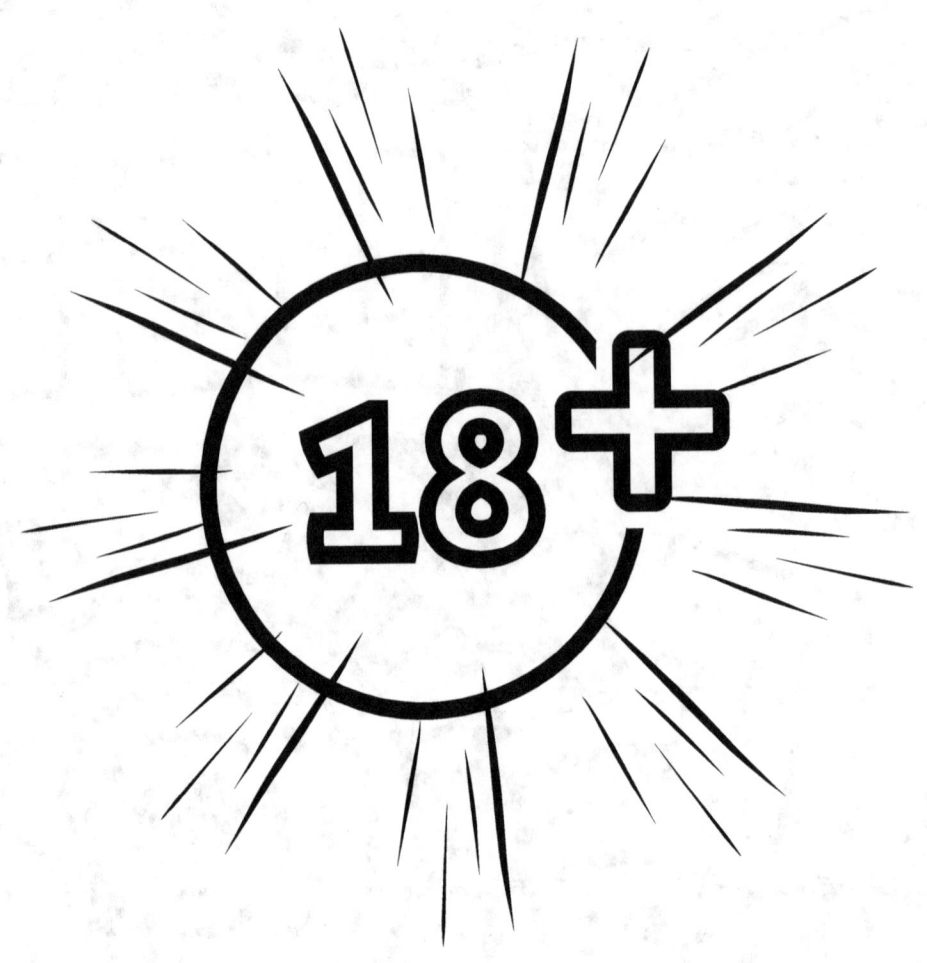

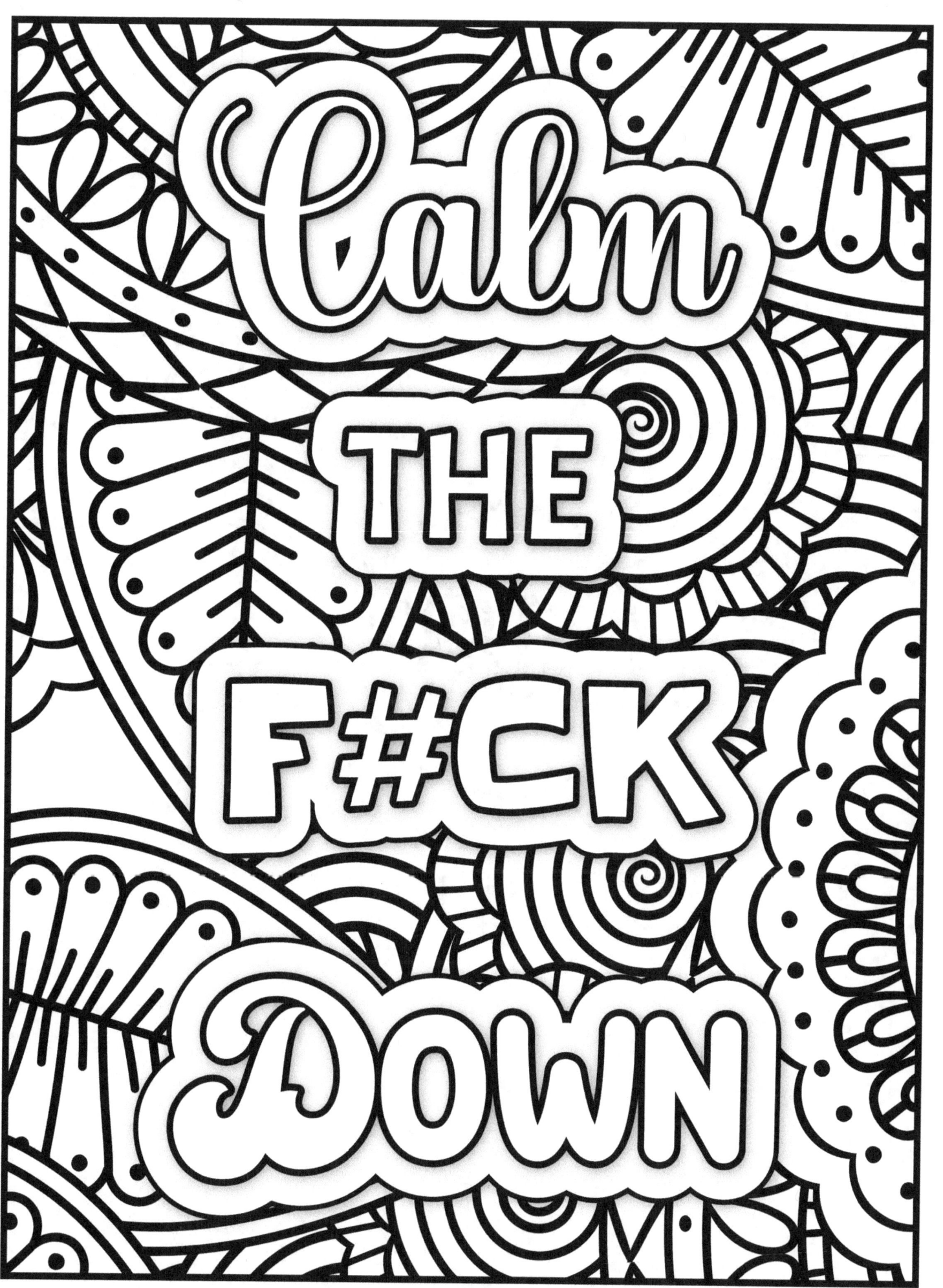

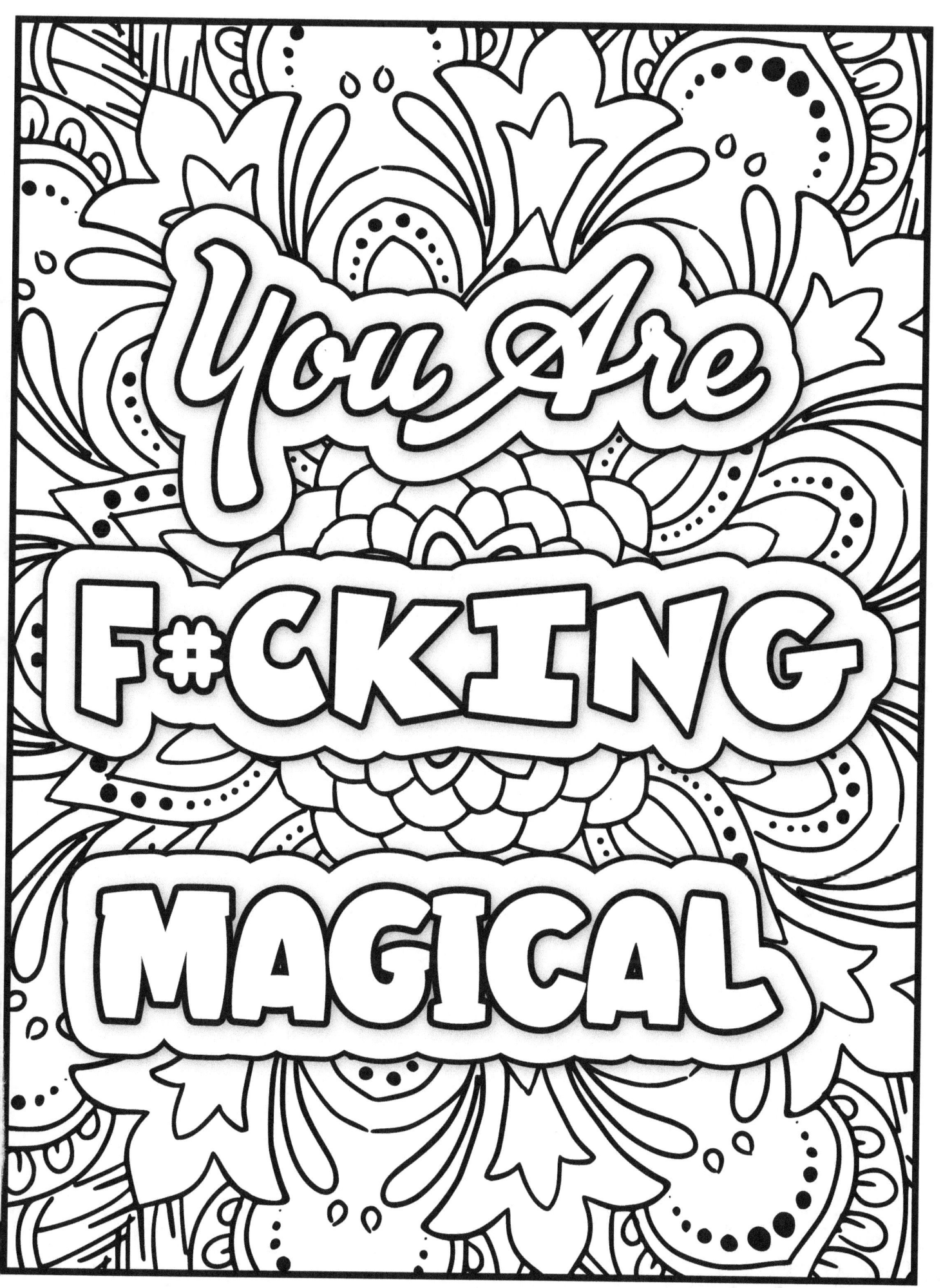

www.ingramcontent.com/pod-product-compliance
Lightning Source LLC
Chambersburg PA
CBHW062222220526
45471CB00009B/3307